To George
my fellow referee

Thank you for your
friendship & loyalty –

May God bless you & the family
with good health & happiness

"Mike"

Cooz

Yours buddy –

ARMEN M. KEUILIAN

THE LIFE AND LESSONS

ARMEN M. KEUILIAN
"I LOVE YOU, MR. K."

Copyright © 2006
ISBN: 1-4243-2513-7

Front Cover Design: Linda Zhou
Back Cover Design: Stella Lee and Debbie Tan
First Edition - 2006
Printed in U.S.A.
For information and address:
armensr@hotmail.com

Dedication of the book

This biography is dedicated to Veronica, my mother, *eem myrig*. I have written about her at length in the book, but she deserves to be set apart to show what a special woman she was. She asked for nothing from this world. For 55 years as our mom and dad's wife, she humbled herself to work relentlessly to make our lives better. She may never have received *all* the recognition she richly deserved on this earth, *even* from her own family. But she's definitely enjoying *all* her riches that were stored up in heaven, for God had seen every single good deed this "saintly" woman had done.

ACKNOWLEDGMENTS

I have many people to thank in the preparation of this biography. Thank you, Nahabed Melkonian, for taking time from your very busy schedule as author, writer and publisher, husband and a father, for selflessly guiding me through the completion of my first book. You are generous with your time and I'm proud to call you a cousin.

Thank you, Pastor Tony Roberts, for being my spiritual mentor for over fifteen years. Over the years, your sermons have truly hit home. You have been a great role model for my two boys, as you have been a good friend to me.

Thank you, Mr. Besta, for giving me the opportunity for employment at the "best school" in town. Without that, I would *never* have met the precious students and their wonderful parents, about whom I've boasted in this book.

In searching for a front and back cover, I briefly mentioned to my eighth graders what I needed. Within a week, I was deluged with some beautiful artistic works. I chose the front cover, contributed by Linda

Zhou. The back cover was generated by Stella Lee and Debbie Tan.

Thank you, young ladies, for your help. You all get A's...and candy, too.

In the book, I have mentioned a few of my students by name to give my story real meaning. That is going to get me into trouble. For in my ten years at El Rancho Middle School, I've had over 3000 students who have given me the inspiration to write this book. I thank them, and I love them all.

Finally, I thank my wife Jeannie for her help in typing this manuscript over and over until it took some semblance of acceptable work. I love you. Keep the tea warm; I'm coming home.

For nearly fifteen years, it has been my privilege to be "Pastor" to Armen Keuilian and his precious family. Actually, we have more than a pastor congregant relationship; we are family. His family is mine, my family is his.

I commend to you this author and book. In it you will find the heart of a loving man who is passionate about his life's calling, being a teacher. Many times I have witnessed the love exchange between "Mr. K" and his students. It can happen any place at anytime. Undoubtedly, he has made a positive and lasting impression on them.

This book offers, also, thought provoking academic challenges to students and parents, and equally important, a most concise written history of the Armenians. Please take note of this oft times negated history. Armen unfolds this history through sharing his family's plight. It is worth knowing.

You will be challenged to persevere through all the circumstances as you read this book. More than that, you will be urged to excellence.

Pastor Tony Roberts
LIFE Church International
Anaheim, CA

I was very fortunate to hire Armen Keuilian. He was not your average new teacher. At 50, he had already been a successful businessman and now he was sitting before me attempting to earn a job at El Rancho teaching Spanish and French. At the interview table, I heard about his work with kids on the soccer field and his dream of becoming a teacher. But most importantly, what I saw in his eyes was passion. This was a man that was committed to his work. This was a man that you would want to teach your child.

An average day in Mr. Keuilian's class includes plenty of interactive instruction in foreign language. But he also shares a healthy serving of what our kids need so badly—lessons on life. He instructs in the rights and   wrongs of life to students that are sometimes not clear on those issues. If a student needs extra help with assignments or needs to talk about a problem, Armen is there.

Over the last several years, Armen has observed the inner workings of life in an American middle school. He is able to share the quirks, the tension and the comedy that is part of teaching teenagers. He is able to share the love and dedication that he has for his students. Yes, I was very fortunate to hire Armen Keuilian.

John Besta, Principal
El Rancho Charter School
Anaheim Hills, CA

PROLOGUE

Hey, can I talk to you? The story I'm about to tell is accurate and true, according to the life that I have lived to date, and not necessarily how history has told it. This contains *my* life, *my* feelings and *my* understanding of *my* experiences... they may be one and the same.

My wife and I were vacationing at a San Diego resort during one of my school breaks. It happened to be Easter Break, or more politically correct, Spring Break. That April 6th morning, as I was reading USA TODAY, my world came crashing down. Gene Pitney had passed away!!! To many, that may mean very little. To me, a part of my being had just died. Who in the 1960's does not remember such great rock-n-roll hits as *Every Breath I Take, Love My Life Away, The Man Who Shot Liberty Valence, Only Love Can Break A Heart, 24 Hours From Tulsa*, just to name a few? Gene Pitney was a true talent among some of the not-so-talented singers of his time. My wife and I had just caught his show in Las Vegas where he was on his way to Europe for a schedule of concerts. If I remember correctly, in his younger years, this musical genius had a 5-octave singing-voice range.

His passing away at 65 isn't all that tragic; we shall all meet our Maker, some day. It's just that my thoughts took me back some 40-50 years to that age of innocence, the good old days, the fifties and the sixties. Yes, I'm one of those Baby Boomers, born in the mid-to-late forties...always looking back as I look forward.

Chapter One

The Good Old Days

In the fall of 1956, in New York, my two older brothers enrolled in public schools, while my twin sister and I attended nearby St. Joseph's Catholic Elementary School. We walked to school and back, a mile or so, each way. Elementary school (up to 8th grade) was fun, even though it was run *strictly* by nuns (pun intended). It was here, at the church steps of St. Joseph's that I met a beautiful twelve year old girl whom I vowed to marry one day. I was only fourteen, myself.

I promoted from St. Joseph's Elementary to begin my high school years. The year was 1961. That was the year the Bronx Bombers won yet another World Series. (That would make five-out-of-six since 1956, wouldn't it, Dr. Payne? He's a colleague, just another frustrated Boston Red Sox fan). Sorry to deviate, but once a Yankee fan, always a Yankee fan. As a matter of fact, our high school, Cardinal Hayes, was only fifteen short blocks (less than 2 miles) from Yankee Stadium.

High school was truly a special time for me. Besides an excellent education, I was schooled in discipline. For some reason, parochial school education is head and shoulders above that of a public school. Systematic training and subjection to authority stands out in my mind as a No.1 priority. A heavy load in studies and responsibility for one's own actions were a close second and third. I clearly remember doing over 4 hours of homework nightly. Weekends were no different. Our teachers were extremely strict in giving us an excellent education. And I thank them for that.

In the fifties and sixties, in private schools, teachers and administrators had full parental cooperation to physically punish any student wrongdoings, even to and from school using public transportation. God forbid we gave Cardinal Hayes High School a bad name.

I remember students caused mischief on buses and subways in New York and the word reached the Dean of Discipline...*Fuhgettaboutit!* Those students were brought in and severely punished. I'm talking about getting whacked (by specially-made rulers) not only on the rear end but also on knuckles and fingertips. I, even *I* got into trouble every so often, often for my thick, curly hair. It had to be a crew cut and nothing more. I was sent home to get a proper haircut more than once if the Dean could just grab the front of my hair. We also had a dress code. Suits and ties were a must – ten below zero or 100 degrees above. And in New York, July and August were sizzlers. One could fry eggs on the sidewalk. Air conditioning? What was *that*?

At times, students would get out of hand at an assembly in the auditorium. The Dean would walk in and he'd yank kids out from their seats and into his office. You could hear a pin drop. Did I mention that my high school was an all-boys Catholic institution, with priests and brothers as teachers? Any way, this same Dean of Discipline, Father Jablonski (we called him Jabo, but not to his face) one time pranced into the auditorium. *The silence was deafening.* From the rear, he yelled out that a citizen had called the school and complained about the behavior of a Cardinal Hayes High student on the bus to school. *"And if that culprit is not in my office within two minutes, he had wished he weren't alive...."* A second later, no less than 20 students sprung from their seats and made a mad dash up the aisles toward his office. That's the kind of discipline I had during my four years at Hayes Penitentiary...I mean High School. Honestly though, those four years were the best years of my educational life. Good times, good education, good friends – even to this day. As an example, Dr. Rick Luceri, one of the top cardiologists in the country today, was a classmate with whom I keep in touch regularly.

Nothing much has changed in forty years, except *everything*. The last half-century has revolutionized the world, especially in technology. Could we have imagined, then, this tremendous progress into digital cameras, cell phones, iPods, the Internet? At the click of a mouse, the whole world is revealed to us in a split second (a little longer with my p.c.). Forget the textbook, the phone, the mail, and television. How *passé*!

Please, don't misunderstand me. There's nothing wrong with progress. Now-a-days, the world could not function without the Internet. It makes me wonder, however, how we ever lived without the computer – just 15-20 years ago. Nevertheless, corporations, schools and households are all heavily impacted by this technological wonder. *I* even use the computer in my classroom, for menial tasks, such as grading and attendance. Whatever happened to calling out names of students and hearing their responses? It takes me six months, I regret to say, to learn the names of all my 250 students.

That's not as bad as what the Internet has *really* offered us recently. In the same newspaper that mentioned Pitney's demise, it told of a United States Federal Homeland Security official, held without bail on 23 felony counts of trying to seduce what he thought was a 14 year-old girl on the Internet. And that same night, on CNN, a 19-year-old boy, at a congressional hearing, spoke about his 5-year exploitation of sexual favors over the Internet, selling his body to predators for what amounted to be hundreds of thousands of dollars, all with the blessing *and* guidance of his father. Yeah, the good, the bad, and the ugly of the Internet. Does your child have

"My Space"? No? Must be behind times...

By now you may have guessed that I'm a teacher. Yes, I teach. I teach Spanish and French at a distinguished charter school in Orange County, California. The community is mainly White, Middle Eastern and Far East Asian – quite affluent. This will be my tenth year of teaching 12-14 year olds. I wasn't always a teacher. So, where should I begin to tell the tale? At the *very* beginning would be a good start.

I was born in the Middle East, of Armenian parents, in an old Biblical town called Joppa (Jaffa), in 1946, the year Israel "reclaimed" its statehood from Palestine. Since then, I might add, not a day has passed without some sort of violence between the two nations – from suicide bombings to mass murders. Have you read the newspapers lately? *War! What is it good for? Absolutely nothing.* I won't take sides here, except to say that in 1948, our family, including thousands of other Christians, had to escape the war-torn area. Some families obtained visas to immigrate to the United States; others went back to Armenia, which was under Communist rule – a bad move. More on this later.

My father, Manuel, orphaned by the Turkish massacres of two million Armenians in the early 1900's, was far more intelligent. Since we didn't make the quota to immigrate to America in 1948, he settled for Jordan, a nearby pro-western Arabian monarchy. Needless to say, we waited for our visas –

7

patiently and hopefully – for approximately eight years, as refugees in that foreign country.

Finally, and through proper and legal procedures, we immigrated to the United States of America, in June of 1956.

Where was I? Oh yes, I wasn't always a teacher. Our family of seven (including four sons and a daughter) finally crossed the Atlantic and entered New York City. One of the most memorable and emotional moments of my life, even at age 10, was staring at the towering site of the Statue of Liberty, as our ship entered the Harbor and docked at Ellis Island.

The American Dream many people "*die*" to attain? We made it - *alive*! We didn't ask for anything more – no welfare, no benefits, and no handouts. We just wanted the opportunity to work hard and start a decent life in the "Land of the Free".

On our ship, there were many other Armenian families, whose final destinations were Boston, Chicago, Detroit and Los Angeles. Ours was New York only because our sponsor, the man who vouched for our goodness, was a U.S. citizen, himself a recent immigrant from Jordan. In fact, my dad and he, for a short time, owned a small automotive parts store back in Jordan.

As I mentioned, we spent about eight, long years in the Capital City, Amman. Amman, Jordan, is probably no larger than the City of Anaheim. It was (and still is) an Islamic country, but Christians were tolerated. I'd go so far as to say that Christianity flourished there. I remember we had both an Armenian Orthodox *and* Catholic Church and School, in the same town.

Chapter Two

The Armenian Genocide

Amman became home to many Armenian refugees, who escaped the massacres of the malicious Turkish Government's planned and premeditated annihilation of a documented two million Christian souls at the turn of the Twentieth Century.

I don't care what you read in history books. And you won't find much at all in American published literature. I know **this** to be true. Decades before the Jewish Holocaust by Hitler's Germany, the Turkish Government planned and carried out a similar genocide of the Armenians living in Turkey. We not only lost 2/3 of our people, but also 2/3 of our land to the Turks. The other third was in the hands of the Russians. Thank God, after all those years of Communist and Turkish domination, we *now* have our own Free Armenia.

You may detect a hint of hatred in me toward our perpetrators. A systematic, premeditated attempt to eradicate a whole race will do that to survivors and their off springs.

What do I mean by systematic?

The plan was carried out to perfection. During the height of the massacres, all Armenian intellectuals, writers, civic leaders, priests and heads of households were rounded up and beheaded or shot to death. Next, teenage boys and young adults were drafted into the armed forces and shot by firing squads. Finally, helpless children, young ladies and older women were forced into a death march through the torturous desert. *That's* what I mean.

Those who know me know that there is not an ounce of hatred in me. Not toward the Turkish people. As a matter of fact, many Turkish citizens, risking their own lives, tried to help and hide Armenians in their homes. The Turkish people were not to blame.

Culpability usually belongs to heads of governments that cause such horrific acts against humanity: Saddam Hussein of Iraq; Adolph Hitler of Germany; and Enver and Talaat Pashas of Turkey.

I don't even harbor any hatred toward the Turkish Government. I just resent the heinous crimes committed against my people, including my grandparents. I never knew them but *how* I can feel their pain. By the way, the Turkish Government to this day has never admitted to doing this horrendous act of violence against our people. In fact, they deny it. They say it happened during World War I and Armenians were aiding the enemy. But this planned annihilation began in 1895, *years* before the war. Furthermore, to cover up their inhumanity, these tyrants have influenced the United States so much so that American history books will not *dare* write a blurb about the incident. Nor will any American president honor his pre-election pledge and publicly condemn the atrocities of the Ottoman Turks.

Why *not*? For fear of losing American air bases in Turkey…and oil. *Plain enough*?

The United States may fold under pressure, but our people will not. Author William Saroyan said it best when he wrote: "You can take away our land and kill our people but you will *never* be able to wipe us off the face of the earth…." I paraphrased the preceding statement to express our people's tenacity, resolve, and attachment to family and church which has enabled us to survive centuries of persecution and discrimination.

Please understand. I'm condemning neither the Turkish people nor Moslems. I know many caring Islamic people, as well as some hideous Christians. *I'm talking about extremists who kill in the name of their god.* However, I know of no loving and just God that will condone killings and reward those who kill, *even* in His name. I know *my* God will not.

My father, may God rest his soul (he passed away in 1986 in California), was a very quiet, somber man all the days that I knew him. Witnessing the beheading of his own parents (my grandparents) would do that to a son. To save themselves, his older brother and he escaped into the woods, lucky to be rescued by the British Red Cross, and consequently placed in an orphanage in Palestine.

My mother Veronica's family fared slightly better, in that, along with thousands of families, every member was forced to march out of Turkey and into the scorching and murderous desert – to perish. *Many did!* If you have the time, I suggest you read a few books written by survivors, such as *Some of Us Survived, by Kerop Bedoukian*, whose loved ones were snatched from them during the treacherous deportation, and beheaded (the male), disemboweled (the pregnant mothers), raped (the young ladies), thrown off cliffs (the old), and left for dead in the desert sands of Syria and Mesopotamia, for vultures and jackals to feast. You won't readily find such books in our public libraries; they **all** have been "withdrawn", if you know what I mean.

The students and teachers at school often ask me, "why do you usually wear black, Mr. K?" Much like Johnny Cash but on a much larger scale, I remind myself *and* those who ask, about the cruelties my ancestors suffered for their faith and religion. I'll make it plain: *Turks are Islam and Armenians are Christian.*

By the grace of God, my mom's family survived. They made it out of Turkey and eventually into Syria and Palestine.

Chapter Three

The Middle East
The Hotbed of the World

In Israel, my father was released from the orphanage at age 16 and began to work at different jobs until he was permanently employed by the British Government as an engineer, a draftsman. He designed roads and highways in Tel Aviv, the Capital of Israel at the time. *That* he did for 22 years. Great Britain controlled much of the Middle East well into the late 40's. Here in a suburb of Tel Aviv, Jaffa to be exact, Pop met Mom and they married in 1934 and began to raise a family.

I don't really know life in Jaffa, (Palestine) Israel. I was born in 1946 and left in 1948. So, from 1934 to 1946, God blessed my parents with many children. My mom's first off springs were beautiful, healthy twins...who only lived 7 months. So suddenly, both died of unknown causes. One moment laughing, and the next, unstoppable crying...and then, silence! Mom could never explain to us why they passed away, without a symptom. "The war," she would murmur. "A*sdoodzo gumken eh*, (it is God's will)." Inexperience and lack of good care, perhaps? A new mom, overwhelmed...?

In the next few years, God continued to bless her with the births of my three older brothers - Vagharsh, Ardash and Shavarsh – all named after Armenian kings. *Oh yes*! Armenia has a very rich and long history. Once a powerful nation, it *even* helped the Crusaders in their quests in the Middle East.

In 1946, Mom had triplets! Yep, I'm the oldest of the three, my twin sister, Zarouhi, being the youngest. The middle child, Yenovk, did not survive the day. Again, you have to understand the circumstances of a mother – *with three very young children* – giving birth to triplets during a war. No doctors! No prenatal or postnatal care. Most children were born at home then, with the help of midwives. *Asdvadz hokeen loosavoreh.* May God rest his soul. No doubt he's in heaven with Mom and Pop, and the first set of twins.

1946! Israel is a new nation, surrounded by hostile Arabic countries, upset by a mandate favored by England, France and the United States: the creation of a new state (Israel) within a nation (Palestine), the Biblical Homeland. *They offered European Jews, who suffered their own treacherous holocaust at the hands of Germany's Adolf Hitler, a passage to Israel.* In doing so, the Western Powers cared little about the

Palestinians who had lived in the region for more than a thousand years.

To tell you the truth, this forever-lasting animosity between two "Biblical brothers", Jacob and Ishmael (Jew and Arab), is mind-boggling...and a shame. And I perceive no foreseeable peaceful solution. On the contrary, I see escalation of war....

Put yourself in the shoes of the Palestinians for a moment. Let's say, for example, that the United States Government designates Florida as a Cuban State. It encourages all Cubans to move there without paying heed to the local Floridians. Even better, in another scenario, imagine that the police come to your home and inform you that you no longer own your home and demand that you share it with intruders. Better yet, Mexico encourages its citizens to enter California, to live and work in places natives must now relinquish. Yes, illegally – without care or concern about the local citizens. After all, California once belonged to Mexico.. What do you think? Too harsh an analogy?

So, back to the late 40's in Israel. We Armenians are Christians, living in a country that is Islam, changing to Jewish. We had no quarrel with either. However, in 1948, during the first major upheaval, the Christians were the ones to suffer. We were asked to leave. No, we *had* to leave to make room for the newcomers. There was no place for us any longer.

Graciously, America opened its arms to the refugees. So did many other nations. However, it wasn't that simple to leave. It wasn't easy. The demand to move was so sudden that our family had to leave town immediately – relinquishing home, household, business and friends. My father told the story of how we were pushed hurriedly into trucks, if we wanted to leave then – somewhat reminiscent of forty years earlier in a God-forsaken place called Turkey, where many (those who weren't beheaded) had to leave all their belongings and march into the devastating desert. This time, however, there was no desert and there were no Turkish soldiers to murder and ravish the refugees.

So we left, with thousands of other Armenians, only to look for a new home, again.

At this time, there was great propaganda from the USSR to have Armenians return to their "Homeland" with the promise of food and lodging waiting upon arrival. My father was an orphan but an educated man. He knew *never* to trust the Communists. After all, they stole a third of our Homeland.

Many gullible Armenians, including my mother's parents and cousins, accepted Russia's offer and made the trip back home. It was a bad and unfortunate decision. Armenia was a satellite of Communist Russia.

From 1948 to 1989, until the fall of Communism, those who returned to Armenia suffered a life almost equal to what Turkey had done previously.

In any case, some went to Russia, some to Armenia, others to the United States and to all corners of the world. Armenians became a scattered people. Our family ended up in Amman, Jordan. Oh sure, we *too* wanted to go to the United States. But we had to wait. There was this matter of visas and quotas. We had to go through legal channels. America was only allowing so many refugees per year, per country. So we waited eight years, yet in another strange land – awaiting our visas and preparing to be physically, mentally and socially ready – to enter the United States of America.

For the first few months in Amman, Jordan, our family lived in a refugee camp, in huts. Soon after, my father found employment, once again designing and drawing roads in Jordan. We moved into a rented home of four brick walls and a roof, and a small courtyard. *No electricity, no gas, no carpeting, no indoor plumbing. None!* It was just a 15' x 15' room for a family of seven – father, mother and 5 children under the ages of eleven.

In Amman, we the children went to an Armenian Orthodox Church and school. Soon after, Mom transferred us to an Armenian Catholic school – she being Catholic. There was no room at the former school because of the influx of other Armenian families.

Amman, Jordan became a large Armenian

community. Now, however, we had to live alongside Arab Muslims.

Armenians are 99% Christian – Orthodox, Catholic and Protestant. In fact, we boast about being the first nation, back in the Third Century, to accept Christianity as a national religion. And overall, we're quite religious. "Wherever there are two or more Armenians," they say, "you will find *two* churches built." The Church is the community center – religious and social.

At the age of 4, along with my twin sister, I was enrolled in Kindergarten, which had 4 levels – 4 years of pre-school. The classes were named after flowers, in Armenian: *dzil, popogh, gogon, dzaghig.* Even at that level, believe it or not, we were exposed to four different languages: Armenian, our Mother Language; Arabic, mandated by the government; English, for its popular appeal; and French, the universal language at the time. Naturally, we also learned History, Math, Science and Physical Education...all this before the first grade.

I remember my early years vividly. They were happy years, replete with social gatherings and celebrations. The Armenian Community was quite large in Amman, with schools, churches and social clubs, centers for both the young and old. Every day, after school until early evening, kids spent time at the club, doing homework, playing ping-pong, foosball, billiards, basketball, and of course, soccer. The closest thing to baseball was a variation of stickball, where the defense would throw the ball and "strike" the base runner to make an out. You would assume we played with a rubber ball. I remember even playing dodge ball, over fifty years ago.

Even though we lived in a mud and brick, one-bedroom-for-seven room, with an outhouse as a toilet (with no seating), I don't remember us being destitute. Yes, we were poor. But *hyrig* (Pop) worked, and *myrig* (Mom) made the best of what he earned. We had *no* electricity (nor heat), just a small courtyard with a faucet of running water. We bathe in a tin tub. At night, we used lanterns with gasoline-drenched-cloth flints to produce light.

Come to think of it, we **were** quite poor, but you couldn't tell by me. I do recall, however, that we received yearly rations of food (rice, wheat, flour, etc.) and used clothing from the American and British Red Cross. We had clothing on our backs, schooling, friends, a roof over our heads and yes, a lot of love – not only from our parents but also from teachers, neighbors and relatives. We were one, big, happy, *poor* community, whose children belonged to one and all. I honestly remember being disciplined by neighbors, as *my* mom would do the same to the neighbors' kids. "It takes a village to bring up a child," the saying goes.

Summer vacations were great – hot and sunny. The children spent most of their days at the Community Club. Our family would also visit relatives in Jerusalem and Ramallah, swim in the salty

Dead Sea and wade through the muddy waters of the Jordan River. Winters were snowy-cold and wet. I clearly remember during the rainy season, we would have a small "brook" running through the middle of our home. We lived on a rocky hill overlooking an old cemetery. In fact, we had to walk through it to get to our house from the main road. At nights, it was a scary "trip" running through the dark and dusty gravesites – kicking up bones of cadavers. Honest truth. But we didn't care; what did *we* know?

I'm sure our parents were distraught, not only about such matters mentioned, but also about the political situation, and our safety. After all, Jordan was an enemy of Israel at the time. I remember, on many occasions, scrambling and hiding under chairs, tables or beds, upon hearing the roar of Israeli bomber planes flying overhead. We feared for our lives. Thank God that they were false alarms – just Israel flexing its muscles.

As a youngster, I couldn't comprehend how a small nation of 5 million people could scare and overpower 100 million Arabs. In short, I imagined that there was no unity among the Arab nations. Not to turn this into a history lesson, but *who* was to lead the attack, and *who* was to relinquish leadership in the war against Israel: Arafat of the PLO, Hussein of Jordan, Assad of Syria, or Nasser of Egypt? They couldn't even get along among *themselves*.

Fifty years later nothing has changed, but a few faces. To be fair, though, let's not forget Israel's big brother (the U.S.A.) in the equation. Our government has always sworn to protect Israel against any and all enemies. Did I mention that since 1946, there has not been a day of peace in the Middle East? It's worth it to reiterate....

To be truthful, the Armenian population did not suffer under the monarchy of King Hussein of Jordan. Even though a Muslim, he was a kind and caring leader. He even took a Christian, Texan beauty to be his queen, Queen Noor – unheard of in those parts of the world, and in those times. He was well educated, pro-Western, and fluent in English. I don't remember the year, but I was in California when he passed away, and I cried the day he died. After all, he was my ruler and king for eight years.

Even though the Jordanian Government tolerated Christians, they strictly mandated that Arabic be taught in our schools. Every so often, government agents would visit, unannounced, to see that their national language was included in the curriculum. *What's so bad about that?* Here was an opportunity to learn yet another language, as a child...piece of cake.

Finally, we were ready to leave Jordan for America, the "Land of the Free". I've got to tell you, as children in Jordan, we used to watch many American movies, with very little comprehension. That's why Western, "cowboy" movies were our favorites, full of action – the likes of *High Noon and Shane*. The American actors were bigger than life to us: John

Wayne, Gary Cooper, Richard Widmark, John Derek, Rita Hayworth and Audey Murphy, whom I dubbed, "The Little Hero". Little did I know that he actually *was* a celebrated World War II hero, in real life. Charlie Chaplin was another favorite of ours. Without uttering a word, he made us laugh and cry interchangeably. We also watched the Little Rascals, in black and white. Not ever having eaten spaghetti, we used to think Buckwheat gobbled down long, swirly worms with delight. *Yuck!* We also believed, as shown on the wide screen, that money grew on trees in America. Who *wouldn't* want to come to America...?

However, the *real* reason why we were leaving the Middle East (Israel and Jordan, respectively) was quite obvious. Well, it became obvious when my father explained it to us. After all, he had seen war and pestilence his whole life. He had seen his parents murdered and his sister disappear at the treacherous hands of the Turks. He lived through WWI and WWII in the hotbeds of Europe and Asia. He experienced the skirmishes between the Jews and Arabs (he lived and worked in Tel Aviv for 23 years). He knew all too well that if we had remained in the Middle East, his four sons would have been drafted either into the Israeli or the Jordanian Army.

Yes, one owes allegiance to the country in which he lives, and that includes defending that country, if need be. However, this was *not* our land, and it was *not* our war. Besides, war is costly, I mean, by way of casualties. Pop and Mom would not have been able to bear the loss of another one or more of their sons. Not after what they had suffered already in their personal lives. *Not after what they had lived through – forty five years of constant bloodshed and danger of imminent war.*

Finally, our visas came through in June of 1956. *Park Asdoodzo;* Praise the Lord. We said our tearful goodbyes to all our relatives and friends at a send-off-farewell party at my uncle's house. Before we boarded ship in Beirut, Lebanon, my father, once more took us through Jerusalem, Jericho and Bethlehem, so that it would always be in our minds and hearts for the rest of our lives. I still envision the Garden of Gethsemane, where Jesus prayed and was betrayed by Judas; the narrow, rocky passageways of Jerusalem, where He carried the cross on His back, having been beaten half to death; Golgotha, the hill where He was nailed to and died on that same cross; and the Holy Sepulcher, a church built on the site of the empty tomb, where Jesus resurrected from the dead on the third day. For a Christian, *that* is the ultimate "Mecca". I'll cherish those memories forever.

Chapter Four

Coming To America

In Beirut, we boarded the Agamemnon, a Greek ship that first took us to Alexandria, Egypt, then through some Greek islands and finally to the city of Pizaeus . There, we disembarked and boarded a much larger ocean liner, Queen Frederica, another Greek ship, much the size and looks of the Queen Mary that is permanently docked at Long Beach, California. We crossed the Mediterranean Sea, passed through the Strait of Gibraltar and sailed into the open waters of the Atlantic Ocean. I had never been on a ship before; it was an absolute delight – a cruise with fine food, entertainment and lodging. Many of us, on occasion, got seasick, but that was expected, I'm sure.

It took us 22 days, I believe, to cross the ocean and hit the shores of Nova Scotia, Canada, and finally our destination, New York City. Thank God, we made it. *We finally made it*! Once we cleared customs at Ellis Island, where the authorities checked our physical and mental health, our sponsor picked us up and drove us to his house in the Bronx.

All we had asked of the U.S. Government was to accept us into this land of "milk and honey". Thank you, America, for offering us also..."Life, Liberty and the Pursuit of Happiness." And thank you, Lord, for getting us safely to our new "home".

We arrived in New York in late June. When we stepped off the ship, my father had only $40.00 in his pocket. It didn't take our family very long to get to "work". None of us, except my father, could carry on a conversation in English. Here we were, in a strange country, with strange people, language and customs. Was it intimidating? *Downright scary*! But we were determined to succeed. Even the youngest in the family, my twin sister and I (at ten years of age) knew not to be a burden to the family. We were resolved to get on our feet rather quickly – with no further assistance from our hosts, the sponsor and the U.S. Government.

My father soon found employment in the same field as in the Middle East. He now worked in downtown Manhattan, designing roads for an engineering firm. At first, it was tough, riding the subway to and from work. But who said it was going to be easy? My nineteen year old brother also began to work, locally, as a mechanic's helper. He really didn't need English to replace generators, starters and brakes on cars. It didn't pay much, but it was a start. Not more than a few years later, after his tour of duty in the Army, he owned and operated his own gas station. The rest of us kids attended nearby schools; classes began in September. Mom did what she knew best – cook, clean and take care of the household.

For the first three months, we lived in one large room, with a small bathroom and no shower. We bathed at the neighbor's, upstairs. This arrangement was a little better than what we had in Jordan. But we did not complain. Soon after, we moved into a tenement building that accommodated the seven of us. This wasn't the happiest place on earth either, for we shared our apartment with rats and roaches. Even though my mom was a very clean housekeeper, the landlord did very little repairs of any sort. That brought many uninvited pests into our abode from surrounding dwellings. New York, in the summer, is almost unbearable. The building had no air conditioning, so we spent our summers "up on the roof", for sun and fresh air. It was a fairly poor neighborhood, with dirty streets and playgrounds. After all, we're talking about the Bronx.

As years went by, we continued school. In the afternoons, each one of us worked to help out the family. I remember my first employment, at 13. I was hanging cleaned and pressed laundry at a French dry cleaner, owned by two Jewish brothers. It must have reached 110 degrees inside the rear of that store. I was paid 50 cents an hour. My second job was delivering the *New York Post* newspaper, door to door. I made $15.00 a week. It was a thankless job. Sometimes, my customers would not pay, weeks on end, and I'd go home with nothing at the end of the week. After all, I had to pay for every newspaper I delivered.

Finally, thank God, at the age of 15, I began working at my oldest brother's gas station in the Bronx, relieving him for 3-4 hours a day after school, while he took a break, only to return to take me home at closing time. Archie (Vagharsh was too difficult to pronounce in the Army), was a workhorse. You may remember that a week or two after we set foot in New York, he began to work. He sacrificed going to school to help the family out, financially. He taught me much about life and hard work. Without saying a word – just with hard work – he made such an impact on me. I worked for him loyally in New York; I continued working with him in Orange County for the next 30 years.

In the early and mid 60's two of my older brothers joined the Armed Forces. The older (Ardash) enlisted and was stationed in Mississippi; the younger (Shavarsh) was drafted and shipped to Viet Nam. Like all households with family members away at war, we were on pins and needles, with our eyes and ears riveted to the television set – daily fearing the worst. During Shav's (short for Shavarsh) year and a half stint in Nam, we received many letters and sporadic phone calls from him, assuring the family that he was well, in the thick of battle in the jungles near Cu Chi, thirty five miles from Saigon. At times he sounded gung ho, and at other times he seemed incoherent and terribly home sick.

I can honestly feel the anxiety of parents and

siblings, awaiting word from their loved ones who are stationed in Iraq and Afghanistan today. I also must say that I have great admiration for those who risk their lives for our country so that the rest of us can live in relative peace. I know it's in the Gospel of John but I can't remember exactly where: *Greater love hath no man than this, that one lay down his life for his friends.*

In June of 1965, I graduated from high school with honors – in the top 35 of my class of 500. I had planned to attend a Catholic college but opted to go to a local city college for proximity. After all, gasoline was at a whopping 29.9 cents a gallon.... That summer, I worked full time at my brother's gas station and learned the ins and outs of running a business. He *saw* that in me and out of the goodness of his heart took me in as a junior partner.

Chapter Five

California Dreaming...A Reality

In September of 1965, at the start of my first year at City College of New York, Ard (short for Ardash) finished his tour of duty in Mississippi and came back home to New York, with his wife and toddler. Soon after, he moved to California with Archie, the oldest brother. They leased a Shell gas station in the City of Westminster and started where we left off in New York. And as I finished my first year of college, I joined them in July of 1966 in Orange County, California, leaving my *fiancée* behind.

Yes, that same gal I met on the church steps, some eight years back.

I continued my education while working a shift at the gas station. This was very difficult for me, since Jeannie, my bride-to-be, was 3000 miles away in New York. She couldn't leave school or her parents to be with me until we were married. So, for one solid year, we telephoned each other daily (day and night), and we wrote to each other almost as often. *There were no free phone minutes in those days*. It got to be so expensive that I thought marrying her would be cheaper. Seriously though, before I had left New York, we set a date for our wedding. I would fly back after my second year of college, marry her in New York and bring her back home with me to the West Coast.

In that one year, it was also very difficult to keep my hands and eyes off of all those college co-eds. *Yeah, I was engaged but I wasn't blind.* Oh, those California girls, the surf... and the music of the Beach Boys! *Too tempting.* While going to school and work, I lived with Archie's family, who kept me in line – most of the time.

Finally, in late July of '67, I flew back to New York to marry my Jeannie (with the light brown hair). She had made *all* the arrangements. All I had to do was put on a tuxedo and walk down the aisle. My two best buddies (Maurice and Rick) from high school were my ushers, along with my immediate brother-in-law, Dominick. The "best man" was a close cousin, Yerchan.

We got married in Long Island, in an Armenian Apostolic Church, in the old traditional style. To this day, my wife says our marriage should have been annulled, in that she didn't understand a word of the marriage vows, mostly done in Armenian. Seriously though, throughout that year of my absence from New York, Jeannie had often visited her mother-in-law (to be), my Mom, and learned to cook all those wonderful Armenian dishes that I ate growing up. You *know* what they say: "To a man's heart is through his stomach...."

What a life ahead of me! I was marrying an Italian and Armenian food *connoisseuse.* I didn't care if I became rich or poor. I couldn't go hungry. "To a man's heart is through his stomach." Didn't I *just* mention that....? By chance, an old 60's song also comes to mind that says, "If y*ou wanna be happy for the rest of your life...get an ugly woman... who can cook...to marry you.* " I tell you, my wife *sure can cook.* Yeah baby, I lucked out 'cause she's a beauty to boot.

So we got married, and had a memorable, large reception, with both sides of our families and friends attending. The next morning, as newlyweds, we flew out to California, on our way to honeymoon in Hawaii. Well, long story short, *that* didn't happen. My oldest brother "gently" informed me that he needed me at work, since I had *already* taken too many days off. No problem. We postponed the honeymoon for a later date.

Chapter Six

A Thriving Career

There's an old Armenian tradition that holds true for most *all* Armenians (and a few other ethnic groups as well). Family members work together, sometimes for life. And family businesses are passed on from parents to children, for generations. For Armenians, it was the garbage, the carpet, the jewelry or the gas station business. Our family was no different. So we worked, all four brothers, side by side, and we built a small empire. Eventually, we bought and completely owned, free and clear, large pieces of real estate, including our workplace. We labored for 30 solid years, running two gas stations, a mini-market and an automotive/tire/towing company. All this, while raising our respective families. Life was good. God was good. He supplied *all* our needs.

I learned very early in life about hard work and responsibilities. The automotive business, for owners, is a difficult job – long hours, and mostly dirty, greasy, manual work. Eventually, I, as the only college educated brother of the four, handled the clerical office work, as well as some mechanical. Work became burdensome.

Oh wow! I almost forgot. After having been married for several years and making all kinds of money, I quit college. But what I *really* wanted to mention is that all the years that I worked with my brothers, leaving my college studies (from 1970-1995), there wasn't a day that I didn't think about going back to finish my education. For 25 years, I felt this large hole in my heart and soul, an emptiness I could not fill nor satisfy. So in 1996, I decided to leave my brothers and the lucrative business, to pursue the completion of my education.

I felt a calling, God calling me to do His work.... After all, *He* gave me all that I had: a beautiful and decent wife, two wonderful boys, a large home in the Hills of Anaheim, and exotic cars (a Rolls Royce and an AMG 1000 Mercedes). *I had it all.* Now it was time for me to give, to pay back.

In 1986, the brothers and I had donated a quarter of a million dollars to build a beautiful Armenian Church in Santa Ana, the Holy Forty Martyrs' Church. It was named in honor of our father *and* in memory of 40 innocent children slaughtered (during the Armenian Holocaust of 1915) by Turkish soldiers, smashing their heads against the four walls of a church.

But that huge donation was not for God. That was for *us*, for *our* name to shine in the community.

34

Now I finally realized that it was time to take care of the "poor (people) in spirit".

You remember that hole in my soul? All those years the Lord was working me, preparing me for something great, something spectacular....

Just to deviate slightly, but to make a strong point, allow me to mention that I often give my students important advice from my own life's experiences. One is this: *Don't ever give up on your education. Get your college degree.* The world can take away your house, your car, and all your belongings and *even*, God forbid, your friends and family. But it can *never* take away your education. Left only with your knowledge, you can restart and build anew. An uneducated person cannot. He or she will blame the circumstances for the situation and be a burden to Society and the State. It does not matter whether you are rich or poor. *Get your education first.*

Let me elaborate on what I had already mentioned previously, from my own experience. In 1967, I got married while I was in college. As you know, I was working with my brothers and doing quite well. Yes, it was difficult going to school during the day, working in the afternoon and playing husband at nights and weekends. But I was making good money. I owned my own home and drove a big car. I had money in my pocket.

Who needed college? After all, one goes to college to get a decent job to make money for a living, right? I was already doing that, *without* a college diploma. So believe it or not, in my senior year at Cal State at Long Beach, just nine units short of graduation with a BA in Foreign Languages, I decided to drop out. I quit because work and marriage demanded more of my time. As I mentioned, I had it all – house, cars, money....

But I just wasn't happy inside.

Yes, that large empty hole in my soul. There wasn't a day I didn't think about it.

There's no doubt that all four brothers were workaholics. At first, we put in seven days a week. We couldn't shut down an automotive center on weekends. Saturday and Sunday are the busiest days, since customers ideally have *those* two days to have their vehicles repaired. Look at Pep Boys. To be successful, you've got to be open and available. So were we.

We worked. I mean *we* worked instead of hiring more employees and managers. Our success in the automotive business was due to *our* working, because we could do the work better than anyone else. We provided personal, caring service. Archie's Tire & Towing became a booming business. After all, our business was mainly service and we were the best at it. Honest, attentive service, with a smile. We had clientele from all over the county. They demanded the services of the *brothers*, and *not* that of careless employees. We owned the business; but the business also owned *us*. Working late every night, I came home tired every night.

Days flowed into nights, nights into days, and weekdays into weekends. Just a vicious cycle.... To make a long story longer, I suggested that we close Sundays, regardless of loss of profits. After a long battle and a few arguments with two of the three brothers, we closed Sundays.

By that time, around 1984, my brother Ard, who was also mingling in real estate sales, quit the partnership. At first, we were angry, but in retrospect, we conceded that he had made a wise decision to get away from this dirty, overbearing work.

Closing Sundays was not enough. Our kids were growing, and lacking our attention and guidance on weekends. You know, little league baseball, soccer, picnics and outings, etc.

There I go again. I demanded we close Saturdays also. *All hell broke loose*! "NO WAY," cried my two older brothers. "That would shatter our business and livelihood." By now we were getting used to the good life. They suggested we hire a trustworthy manager to keep the place open on weekends.

OK with me, as long as I didn't have to work. Long story short, the weekend crew robbed us blind. During the week, our regular customers used to tell us about the shenanigans going on, on weekends, while the "owners" were away. So we fired the weekend crew and reverted to closing shop on Saturdays and Sundays – regardless of our financial loss. At least, we had "peace of mind".

Getting back to me, I *still* wasn't happy at my job, even working just five days. The pressure on me was overwhelming. As I mentioned, I ran the clerical end of the business, with the help of a secretary, while still helping out in the shop area. I also handled the paper work for all our other businesses, *and* the IRS. If you own a business, you'd know what I mean. Furthermore, I had the responsibility of keeping the status quo of the luxurious life we all led – on weekends.

We never gave in to the idea of "hiring more and working less." Why would we? What would we do then? Go home and play with our kids? Do "honey-do's" for our wives? Seriously, expand the business with franchises, like Discount Tires? We could have, but we were mentally and physically exhausted by then. Why add more work?

I can shamefully say that in all the twenty five years of working together at Archie's Tires and Towing, my brothers *hardly ever* took a week off for vacation. And I, feeling guilty, may have taken four or five, at the most. Did I not tell you we were workaholics?

Chapter Seven

A Beautiful Home and Family

Nevertheless, "to add a little excitement to my life", I got involved in real estate and obtained a broker's license. I even worked nights and weekends. I did very well, but again, it kept me away from my family. *The richer one gets, the more one wants.* Finer things in life cost plenty of money. So we moved from a modest home in Huntington Beach to a mansion in Peralta Hills of Anaheim – a seven-car garage, one acre land, fifty-three fruit and palm trees, an indoor/outdoor pool and a tennis court. Quite secluded. *It was the perfect home in which to raise kids.* Our two boys went to excellent local schools in a middle-to-upper class community. All was well, again. Or so I thought.

A very large house has very large upkeep and expense. Even though living in this house was the best years of our family life – with good friends and neighbors – it put a great strain on me, mentally and financially. Every penny I made from the automotive and real estate business would go into the mortgage and maintenance of the house.

In the twelve years that we lived there, we repaired the pool and the tennis court three or four times – for major cracks. Our house was built on a slope and on soft soil. Even a very expensive 6-foot retaining wall around the property did not keep the house from cracking and slipping.

To make matters worse, my wife and I, driving to a funeral one late afternoon, got into a horrible car accident on the 5 Freeway. It did major damage to the Mercedes, but worse, it left my wife with terrible back pains that she suffers intensely, even to this day. She had been under the care of many a chiropractor and physical therapist – to no avail. It would hurt her just to walk up the stairs in that tri-level home. She'd go to bed crying, and wake up in tears.

Well, that did it!

Finally, and regretfully, we sold the house to a gentleman who demolished the residence to rebuild a home to his liking. Thank God for a quick sale. However, even a million dollar home (in the mid 1980's) could not bring us the happiness we were seeking. I *even* sold the AMG 1000 Mercedes *and* the Rolls Royce. I didn't want any part of that "rat race" any longer. One more proof that money and personal "stuff" does *not* guarantee happiness on its own.

We didn't move too far, however. In fact, we moved to a smaller, tract home a few blocks from my present job. It is a beautiful home with an exquisite panoramic view that warms my heart each time I look out. What more can I ask for in life?

Chapter Eight

Back To School

I mentioned my present job as a teacher. "How and when did that happen," you say? Do you remember that great big void in my heart I keep mentioning? Well, I prayed many a late night to God for peace of mind, guidance...and understanding. "Lord, what is it that you want of me?" I'd cry out in the wee hours of the morning. "What is it that you want me to do?"

GO BACK TO SCHOOL. FINISH YOUR EDUCATION. GET YOUR DEGREE. TEACH THE LITTLE CHILDREN.

"Teach them what, Lord?"

While in college, I had no idea what I wanted to be. Oh yeah, languages came easy to me, being a Middle Easterner. Did I mention that in my family, including my dad and mom, we actually spoke 8 languages – Arabic, Armenian, English, French, Hebrew, Latin, Russian and Turkish...and Spanish? That makes nine, no? Most of them we spoke very well. So, I thought, how about pursuing *that*?

Languages!

I had studied Latin and Russian in high school and college. After the imminent threat of Communism subsided in the late sixties, I did not see a need for Russian, even though I could carry on intelligent conversations with my Russian/Armenian brother-in-law, Levon, my twin's husband. Furthermore, since I had given up the idea of being a priest, a wish of every Catholic high school administration (I'm being sarcastic), I dropped Latin after the second year of college. Don't get me wrong. The six years of Latin helped me immensely in mastering French and Spanish...even English. Furthermore, I'm proud to say that I read and translated a great portion of the Iliad and the Odyssey from Latin into English.

I loved studying French, "the language of love". In high school, my two best friends, Rick Luceri and Maurice Masson, whom I still cherish, were fluent in French. Both had frequently visited France; the former was a full-blooded Frenchman. I was a bit jealous, so I studied the language on my own and took five years of it in college. I loved it! It was to be my major (to teach, perhaps). However, being in Southern California, I saw very little need for its use. So, I concentrated on Spanish, alongside French.

I had no time for fun or frolic in college. I was married and working. I took my studies seriously and wanted to finish up as quickly as possible. So in the spring of 1970, I thought I would graduate. Having applied for graduation, I was told I was nine units short of getting my diploma. *WHAT?* I was furious, I had done *all* they had asked me to do in the four years and now I needed to put in *another* semester? *NO WAY!* I was burnt out. "That's it," I told my wife. "I'm quitting. Who needs it? I'm already making more money than any college graduate."

That's the way it happened. I had no one to advise me otherwise. I wouldn't listen, anyway. My brothers at work were happy to see me quit, so that I can put more hours, working full-time. *A VERY BAD CHOICE.* I'm confessing now that ever since that day, and every day since, I was sorry for making such a stupid decision.

Yes, I was making good money. Yes, I had a nice home, cars and somewhat of a celebrity status in the community. In addition, in the late 70's and the early 80's my adorable wife presented me with two wonderful boys.

I was on top of the world!

But life has a funny way of bringing one to the realization that money and fame are not everything. Adulation and people's respect mean something but they don't measure up to too much, compared to real happiness within.

Well, after some twenty five years of working, raising a family and building a small empire in business, I decided finally to go back to school, get my diploma and degree and listen to that "still voice" within me. I needed to fill that barren space. *That* would truly make me happy in life. And my wife was very supportive, as always. So, in January of 1996, I enrolled at Cal State Fullerton to finish my BA degree in Spanish. Those nine units that I was lacking actually turned out to be thirty five. *Some recent stipulation made many of my hard-earned credits obsolete.* I had to retake new required general courses alongside the nine I lacked. No problem. I was determined and set to handle whatever obstacles came my way.

Yeah, right! How was I going to accomplish such a feat at age 50? "Go back to college and pick up where I left off some 25 years ago.... My brain could not handle the daily responsibilities of family, work *and* school. Not at *that* age.

Let's take school as an example. The workload was *so* intense that I knew I could not do it – not on my own strength. I just did not have the stamina and the brain power to be able to study and retain the daily workload thrust upon me. College work was not easy, if I were aiming to get serious about my studies. I wasn't there to look for a good time or a future wife. I already had that, and more.

Many nights, I would cry out to the Lord in desperation, wanting to quit. But the Holy Spirit would always remind me to lean upon Him and trust Him, "For not by *my* power but by *His* will... will I accomplish the desires of my heart...." After all, He assured me once before, in the still of the night, to make the change in my career and *He* would guide me.

God would never give you a burden, any more

than you can handle.

If it were not for the grace of God who gave me the fortitude and the faith to carry on, I would never have made it. I *never* lost faith...and He rewarded me for my steadfastness.

After a year and a half of difficult and diligent studying (late into the night and early in the morning), I graduated with a 3.87 GPA – CUM LAUDE. Of *all* the classes I took in college, I had only a couple of B's and the rest were all A's. On graduation day, while walking up on stage to pick up my diploma from the Chancellor of the University, I felt like a 22 year-old graduate with all the weight of the world lifted off of my shoulder. I had finally accomplished what I had set out to do – thirty one years earlier.

Chapter Nine

I Found My Calling

I'm happy to say that this is my tenth year teaching, and I'm as excited about it today, as I was the first day I walked into my classroom – ten years ago. I"*m ecstatic about it!* I honestly can't wait to get up in the mornings to get to class. I can't wait for weekends to end, for Mondays to begin. Vacations are too long.... I must be crazy. *That's* funny. That's what my friends and relatives used to say. "How could you leave such a well-paying job to put up with 12-14 year-old brats?"

Soon after I was hired to teach, I realized what that *void* in my soul was.

It was to teach.

Not just to teach Spanish or French. Any college graduate with a teaching credential can do that. I knew now why God had chosen me to teach. Spanish and French were only tools to get close to the hearts and minds of our very precious, impressionable, young people. It very well could have been English or History, subjects I found intriguing in high school and college. It wasn't only to teach languages, but much, much more than that.

The school I teach at is El Rancho Charter School, a middle school, nestled in the hills of East Anaheim, a middle-to-upper class community. Our school demographics are quite diverse. We have children from almost every ethnic background, predominantly White, Middle Eastern and East Asian. Generally speaking, the Asian students excel in their studies because of parental guidance and values. However, the white students, many with multiple parents, *also* do quite well. A lot has to do with the child's background and motivation. And a lot more has to do with proper education.

This is where I came in. When I first started teaching, I had very little teaching skills. Sure I took numerous "instructional classes". That's what the credential program is all about. However, a piece of paper (a credential certificate) does not make the holder a teacher. In my case, I came in on my ability and background as a leader both in the community and the work place, with love and compassion for children. With those qualities, I jumped head first into my teaching. Ah yes, equally important, I knew my subject matter well and had (still have) a passion for the languages I taught.

Teaching (Spanish and French) at El Rancho, in Anaheim Hills, is the best thing that ever happened to our family. This community is a great place to live. Both my sons, Armen Jr. and Aram, attended local schools, including El Rancho, for their junior high school years. *Amazing!* I remember meeting their teachers, way back in the early 1990's at PTA meetings and Open Houses. Many of those teachers are still at El Rancho, now teaching with me. It was a great school then, and it's a greater school now.

We've gone through a few changes. Having become a "Charter School" has made us somewhat independent of the school district we're in. That was a good thing for our school.

The faculty and parents now decide what is best for our students. After all, who is better qualified to make such decisions? I dare say that our school is the best school in its category in the county, if not the state. We have won numerous state and national academic awards. Parental support is at its peak and our teaching and clerical staff is second to none.

I *love* this school and I *love* my students. There is not an hour that goes by without someone yelling out, "I love you, Mr. K." There's not a day that goes by that I fail to mention how much I love *them*. Between classes, many scribble down "I love you, Mr. K" on the chalkboard or say it to my face, as they hurriedly leave to their next class. It's quite normal at nutrition and at lunch breaks, for several students to run up to me for a hug – boys and girls – even ones who don't take my classes.

Yes, I know. I know all about teacher-student relationships that go on in schools. I know it's not proper to touch students – at all. At the same time, we're told over the PA system to smile, show compassion and hug someone. *And I do.* It is very possible that *that* hug, and a kind word may save the life of a child distraught over home or school issues. Not too far fetched, is it? I've received many a note from students to that effect, thanking me for good, timely advice. Some of our kids are in dire need of a hug and a word of love, Agape (Godly) love, and a genuine concern for their welfare.

The Internet and television are full of negative messages. There are ample opportunities for older people to prey on the young. Our newspapers daily write about teachers, coaches or administrators molesting and violating our young. *SHAME ON THEM!*

Forgive me; I ought *not* to pass judgment. That is not my place. Thank God that there's law and order in our civilized society to incarcerate those with moral decay. And thank God there *is* a God who is the ultimate Judge in such matters. Anyway, let's not dwell too long on the negative.

I tell my students that I'm not here just to teach them Spanish or French. Any person with credentials can do that. That's not to belittle the position, believe me. I'm saying that it takes much more than knowing your subject matter to become a good teacher. I consider myself a *teacher* – much more than just an instructor. Unfortunately, we have seen too many of the latter who come and go, work *just* for the money and care *less* about the school and its students.

Who suffers? The children do. I'm proud to say that I have had only two major jobs in all of my working days – the long stint with my brothers (35 years) and my present teaching job for nearly ten years. Oops! I'm giving away my age; but that's no problem. I give that out readily in class. After all, we daily celebrate happy occasions and birthdays, with songs and presents (balloons, stuffed animals and candy).

Speaking of candy, I'm known in school as the Candy Man. Yes, I know that candy is not good for youngsters, especially with this obesity hype going around. Nevertheless, I give away candy freely. It's a great incentive *and* reward for achievement. And it's about building character and self-esteem. It just works; whatever it takes.

These kids are wonderful human beings.

They are fantastic!

Sure, a few have some issues and problems – family, personal, peer – that they act out. That's quite normal and expected, if not accepted. It's our job, as teachers, to recognize and help solve them.

Our responsibility is to give our students a well-rounded education, with the help of their parents and guardians. It is worth repeating: "It takes a village to bring up a child." In retrospect, didn't I mention that in the Middle East the *whole community* raised us children? Here some fifty years later, it *still* holds true.

Balance is the key to everything. Balance in

food and in education. Forget the food (I must be hungry) for a moment. In education, our students must have knowledge of many things going on in this world. Learning History without current events is useless. Reading English books without a handle on grammar is wasteful. Studying a foreign language without its use is mindless.

How many parents have taken 4-6 years of Spanish, French or German in their school days and can hardly remember two words today?

Education is an on-going experience. You can never have enough. I teach my students that it's the only asset they have that cannot be taken away from them – once they've achieved it.

Chapter Ten

Life Lessons

I don't forget my students even after they graduate. Oh, I may forget their names now and then, here and there, but I always remember their faces. At times, I chat with them on line, just to let them know that I'm there for them, in time of need. And they often return to El Rancho to visit me, and other favorite teachers. What an honor! What an honor to be part of a school that has such wonderful and caring teachers whose previous students take the time to revisit.

Every June, many of my students tearfully say their goodbyes with a hug, and promise to be back to visit. The amazing thing is that many *do* – throughout their high school and college years. The names are endless, such as Alex C., the QB sisters (Lauren and Ashly), Kat and Vica M., Michael S., Allen C., and Semhar D. In my classroom, I have this very large collage of pictures (in the shape of a heart) of present and previous students. They feel a sense of belonging to see themselves in my "Heart".

No, I don't consider myself perfect, if that's what you're thinking. I don't pretend that at all. "I'm *not* perfect," I tell my students. "I'm *near* perfect," as I stand *next to* one of my kids. And I illustrate the Spanish preposition, *cerca de,* meaning *near (to). Yo estoy cerca de Sarah.* Get it? I am near Sarah; I am near "perfect". Yes, it sounds corny, but I use lines as that to keep my students amused in a rather unpopular subject. It's unpopular only because the language is unfamiliar to them. So I try to make every class exciting and interesting. I sing, I yell, I whisper. I use humor, when necessary. I stand on a chair when I have to emphasize a crucial point. I wear a colorful poncho and a huge sombrero to keep them entertained – whatever it takes to keep out boredom and keep in interest.

One of my sayings in class is "Keep Alert, Alive, Awake and Aware." This holds true not just in the classroom, but also out in the world. At their early (teen) age, many students are distracted by the smallest of disturbances in the classroom. For example: a fly (God forbid, a bee), a sneeze, a TA entering class with a note from the office. Forget about note writing, text messaging, pulling hair (yeah, it still goes on), chewing gum, day-dreaming (very popular). In all this, they lose focus of the instruction by the teacher.

Hey, it's a tough age. Their attention span, at times, is equal to their age – in seconds. Thirteen years old = thirteen second span of attention. "Keep quiet" to them, means to be silent for 12-14 seconds.

There *needs* to be focus, and a good teacher must keep the subject matter interesting and fun to hold their attention. For example, a week ago, we learned a song about 15 different animals and the sounds they make in Spanish (the sounds are different in English). It was hilarious. We followed up by playing "Animal Bingo" to review these animals for an upcoming test. I put on my Mickey Mouse hat and ears for fun. The kids had a ball. The winners were many, and all received rewards – yep, lollipops. Was there learning? I'll bet....

Now, I mentioned that alertness and awareness must also carry over to outside of the classroom. I urge them to be aware of their surroundings, even in a simple task as walking to and from school. I advise them to stay away from the enticement of petting a cute doggy or the offerings of candy from strangers, on foot or in cars. "Keep alert," I say. "Pay attention to what's going on around you. Don't be paranoid about it, but be cautious at all times – at home, in school, in a parking lot, in the street or in a park. Stay awake so you can stay alive."

To some, these words may be disturbing to hear, but they may save a life. *And it did,* last Tuesday. Three students (one of them from my class) were walking home after school and they decided to cross a busy thoroughfare, against the light. As they all made it to the center divider, one of them dashed into the second half of the boulevard, unaware of a car quickly approaching on her right. *My* student, Charlotte, being alert, yelled out for her to stop and wait. Too Late! Today, that "jaywalker" is in intensive care with multiple, internal, broken body parts. Thank God she's alive! A lesson to be learned about awareness...and obeying laws.

I heed them to act first when at risk with strangers. "At the first sign of danger, *run* (the other way), *scream*, or *kick* (where it hurts)," I exhort them. "This is no time to be kind to strangers. Use common sense. Walk across the street when you sense danger, and walk with friends, whenever possible. Such alertness will save future hardships."

Let's go back to "perfection", which I certainly lack. *He without sin cast the first stone.* None of us is perfect; only God is. Even though I'm not perfect, I *am*, however, a perfectionist. I instruct my students, "if something is worth doing, do it *well*! Complete the homework assignment; don't just do it partially. Study for the exam seriously, without the "blasting" music. Research the project fully, not superficially."

At times I get angry when students act up and ignore simple rules or instructions. Yes, I'm quick to anger, but I'm quicker to apologize. Many times I've asked forgiveness for having "hurt" someone's feelings, even unknowingly. I've often apologized when it wasn't even *my* fault.

Five years ago, about midyear, I had a newly arrived 13 year old student in one of my Spanish classes. This period was truly a fun class with so much love and joy permeating throughout. "Sean" was new to the school; he knew no one. He felt left out. I sensed that and tried hard to get him involved. However, instead of joining in, he decided to take it out on me by writing obscenities in class textbooks. Book after book, I found four letter words hurled at me, personally. To be perfectly certain, I compared his test penmanship to that in the books. *Bingo!* I confronted him on this and he became belligerent. His counselor and I called home to let the parents know of his misbehavior. Lo and behold, we discovered the reason for his misconduct! A drunken grandma was the guardian of this child. His father had been incarcerated for a criminal offense and the mother had left home, for good.

The grandmother, at this point, became quite defensive and abusive. She accused me of racism and threatened to sue me for false accusation. She would take me to the District Board. She would bring in handwriting specialists. She would "have my job." She also demanded that I apologize to her *and* the child. The counselor, being supportive of me, took me aside and asked if I would like to pursue this. I knew I was in the right and that *I* was the victim. However, I saw a greater victim here, a troubled boy who had no one to love him or take care of *his* needs. Sensing an opportunity to get close to this child, I humbled myself and apologized to them both. Consequently, I took the boy under my wing. I showed him *all* the love I could muster. I became his confidant.

When Sean got into trouble at school, the office

would call me to resolve the issue. I remember one early morning, his counselor called me because Sean refused to recite the Pledge of Allegiance. "What's the problem, my man?" I asked, as I put my arm around his shoulders. "Hey dogg," he replied, "They put my dad in jail and they want me play nice." He was an angry little boy. He needed counseling; more than that, he needed love and understanding.

Fortunately, I'm not the only one that is alert to these individuals who have gone astray. For it's our job, as teachers, to bring them back into the fold, so to speak. Our Pastor Roberts' message last Sunday was exactly on this point. It was Father's Day, and he laid it down hard and heavy...as usual. It pertained to a father and his lost child, but the analogy holds true to a teacher as well.

As to a father, any one can have a child but how many can *really* be fathers? To be a father, one must be protective, compassionate and loving... and forgiving.

Luke 15 says it best (paraphrased): "Do not disown your child...seek him...open your arms...love your child...do not judge...just love him." After all, didn't the shepherd leave his flock to go and find the "lost lamb" and joyfully put it on his shoulders and bring him home?

Dad, you are the projection of what your child will be. He looks up to you. Love him with unconditional love. We as teachers can do the same: *Seek that one child who's astray and bring him back into the fold – lovingly.*

Near the end of this school year, the weather was somewhat hot and humid. As the bell rang to end lunch, I had a bit of water left in my bottle. I'm a practical joker. As I was walking to class amid a crowd of students, I sprinkled just a bit on the kids behind me. It was a refreshing feeling for some students, with much laughter.

One student, however, took the opportunity to get back at me – with a full bottle of green Gatorade. Coming up behind me, he poured the whole thing over my head. I did not even *know* this child by name. My first reaction was of sheer anger; but I wouldn't *dare* strike the boy...this immature child. The students around me were stupefied, knowing that such behavior on his part would undoubtedly cause an immediate suspension. I thought about it for a moment and counted (silently) to ten. The child obviously made a grave mistake in judgment. In my heart, I forgave him. At the end of the day, I reported the incident to his counselor and let it go at that. *I wasn't out for revenge.* It made for a good lesson in humility in my classes for the next few days.

Chapter Eleven

Best Friends

I have a poster in my classroom that I picked up from the School District Office, ten years ago. It lists "Ways to Resolve Problems" with others by: sharing the problem, apologizing, compromising, using humor, ignoring, walking away, etc. I have a whole lesson plan in both languages on this topic. I also show the movie, *West Side Story,* one of the most entertaining *and* educational movies that plays out what can happen when people do not resolve problems peacefully. It can escalate to tragedy.

"If someone's bothering you, just punch his lights out," a boy yelled out. "That's what my dad told me to do." "Okay," I conceded, "If you don't mind a suspension, or worse, Juvenile Hall *and* a lawsuit." "But Mr. K," a girl questioned, "why should I say *I'm* sorry when *she* was the one who said those bad things about me?" Good point.

Here's a true story that happened not even a week ago. At lunchtime on the outside campus, two young ladies that I knew to be close friends were making a big scene arguing, pointing fingers, crying and threatening. At first, I thought to myself, "girlie stuff". Don't interfere; it will blow over.

Instead, it blew up! They got angrier and louder...

"Cat fight!" I heard a boy yell out from the gathered crowd. I finally stepped in. "Girls," I intruded, "I don't have you as students, but I know that you are best friends. Don't hurt each other by making accusations and hurling insults that you'll regret tomorrow. Forgive each other. Hug and make up. You'll be glad you did." I walked away. The next day, as I was monitoring the same area, I heard a call. "Mr. K, you were right about us yesterday," one of the girls yelled out. "Yep," I responded, "never lose your friendship with someone so near and dear. It's too precious." I continued my beat.

Along the same lines, I often notice "best friends" in and out of the classroom. For example, two female classmates would be "hanging" together often, hugging and laughing at nutrition and lunch. "Mr. K, this is my best friend. We're going to be best friends forever," one would boast. In jest – and there's always truth in jest – I'd make a bet with them that their close friendship would not last passed the second year of high school. I would explain the meaning of true friendship, in contrast to "similar interests" friendship. I ask them, "would you give up your warm and cuddly bed at 2 o'clock in the wee hour of the morning, to come to the aid of your best friend?" Silence! At this juncture, I would invite the whole class into the discussion, just to get them thinking.

You might think that it's too early in life to lay such a heavy thought in their minds. However, I want them to anticipate and accept "break-ups" should they occur, even as early as high school. Such reasons as "the opposite sex", sports, new friends and other interests, may separate them.

And that's all right. It's quite normal; it's part of growing up.

I also advise them that, throughout their lives, if they can count their "friends" on one hand, they should feel blessed. I share with them that, personally, I only have a handful of true, close friends – ones that I can rely on, unconditionally.

I have such a friend in Robert, and I love him dearly. Robert likes to drink. I don't love him any less. I love him for who he *is*, not what I want him to *be*. We grew up together in the Middle East. Actually, we separated our ways for a while, as we both migrated to the United States – he to Boston, and I to New York. We finally reunited in California. He lives in Northridge, 70 miles away. He would do *anything* for me, and I'd do the same for him – absolutely. We're as close as brothers.

Over the ten years of teaching, I've won some bets and I've lost a few. Kids take me seriously about friendship. Take Noël and Danielle, for instance. They set out to prove me wrong. Long story short, they continued their close friendship in the first year of high school. However, soon after, they had other encounters and interests that naturally separated them. Occasionally, I'd see one or the other and ask about their relationship. One went the athletic route (quite a basketball handler) and the other, into service clubs and activities (a gifted fundraiser at the age of 16). Soon after high school, they "reconnected" and stayed best friends once more. *Wow, that is awesome!!!* I think I owe them a dinner; I'll be eating crow.

Chapter Twelve

Who's *Your* Role Model?

As a teacher, I can't be mad or stay mad (for long) at my students. Yes, at times they are lazy, indifferent, mischievous, obnoxious, uncaring, down right selfish...please *stop* me!!! ...And weren't we all, at that age. Furthermore, I can't teach them to be forgiving, if I'm not forgiving...them. Kids pick up quickly on hypocrisy.

A quick side bar on forgiveness: Forgiving someone does not make the forgiver any "holier". *One does not get extra kudos for that kindness.* It is to be a natural act to forgive. Even through a selfish motive, it lifts a great, big burden off of the one that forgives.

Many teachers (and parents) say, "Do as I *say* and not as I *do*." I disagree. *My philosophy is: not to chew gum, show anger, use profanity, smoke or drink alcohol in front of my students.* I don't smoke and I rarely drink. However, even when we go out to a local restaurant, my wife often reminds me to stick to a Coke and not to order hard liquor.

There's not a weekend one or several students of

mine will not recognize me in a public place, and run up for a hug. Could be you imagine if I had a drink in my hand, after what I teach in class about smoking, drinking and drugs? It's only a small sacrifice.

I tell my students, "Do as I do."

"That's carrying it too far," you might say. I say, "No!" Children are very impressionable. They mimic. They do what you *do* and not necessarily what you *say*. That's part of teaching. If you want to smoke or drink, do it at home or go across town. It's only a small price to pay....

We certainly don't want our professional athletes and entertainers (movie stars) to be our children's role models – those that hop from one marriage (bed) into another, at a whim. For them, it's as easy as buying a new (or "used") car.

In actuality, *we* are their role models. Whether we like it or not, they see *us*; they look up to *us*. They mimic *us*.

Here's another true story. I was out with the wife and a few close friends (yeah, Robert and his wife) at a restaurant 60 miles from home, one weekend. The next day in class, a young girl excitedly cried out, "Mr. K, I saw you yesterday at the Cheese Cake Factory in Marina del Rey, but I didn't want to bother you." And a month ago, I was in San Diego (100 miles away) with family, celebrating a birthday. Shopping for sunglasses at a store, suddenly, I got a big bear hug...from a former student of mine! Need I say more about our conduct, as teachers, in and out of the classroom?

And along these lines, I teach my kids about respect, honesty, integrity, compassion, honor and... "the greatest of them all, love." I demonstrate these virtues daily, in the school environment. I hold doors open for my students. I pick up their dropped pens and pencils. I rush them a tissue in emergencies. I ascertain certain physical hardships and mental anguishes, and I provide immediate relief, with a kind word or two. Other times, I overlook minor offenses, not to embarrass them. I live what I teach, and I want to be a good example. And many actually listen to the advice I give, which usually coincides with Principal Besta's daily, morning "Words of Wisdom" over the loudspeaker. And he *always* ends his announcements with, "...Make it a great day, or not; the choice is yours."

Chapter Thirteen

Don' t Be a Yo-Yo

I receive many notes and letters from my students during and near the end of the year. Many notes come from parents, as well. They thank me for being a "great" instructor in French or Spanish, *and* for teaching "the important things in life," as they put it. Just tonight, I was chatting on line with one of my former students, Sheila Shalom. In conversation, she mentioned that she may not have listened much to the Spanish I instructed in class, but she *still* remembers *all* the life lessons I taught. Don't let her fool you; she was an "A" student all year long. It warms my heart to see that I'm actually accomplishing what I set out to do in my second career – touch the hearts and minds of the "little people".

Ah, the rewards of teaching....

That's why I teach. It's my responsibility to teach them right from wrong, about consequences for good, as well as bad deeds. How else will they learn? They *can* learn through making mistakes. It's good to learn from one's own mistakes; but it's much better (and less costly) to learn from the mistakes of others. They're only 12-14 years old, for crying out loud. You don't want them to learn from television, do you? Why do we get so upset with children, when they do wrong? Do we get angry with babies as they're growing and learning? Well, here are grown-up babies...

Don't get me wrong. Teaching invariably necessitates discipline, *discipline with love*. That's one of my life's mottos. I applied that in my own family, raising two boys. And I do that *now* in school. Ask any student or administrator. I run a tight ship in my classroom. I'm of the Aretha Franklin mind set. *R-E-S-P-E-C-T... means everything to me.* For example, when adults or other teachers walk into my classroom, my students know to *stand* and be *silent*, to show respect. It's not a show; it's the right thing to do.

Furthermore, I don't tolerate unnecessary distractions during teaching. Spanish and French are tough enough on their own, being foreign languages. I don't allow disinterested kids to take away learning from the serious students – those making a gallant effort to comprehend the matter at hand. While it's time for one student to shine, I don't allow another to "steal" the limelight. I teach my students that not every thought from the brain must flow out of the mouth. There's time for each student to be recognized. Patience is a virtue. One must use the "open and shut" valve attached to the pipeline that connects the brain to the mouth....

Another concept that I'm trying to get into their

hearts and minds is the idea of **giving.** This is quite difficult, since all their young lives, they have been bombarded (through the media) to think *only* about themselves. In fact, this "new age" nonsense is all about oneself – one's own self. Whatever feels good to *me*. It's about *my* hair, *my* body, and *my* needs. I do what *I* want, what *I* like, what *I* feel and what *I* need. "I" is properly translated into Spanish as *yo*. So I admonish my 12-14 year olds not be *yo yo's*.

"God has blessed you, all your lives," I say somewhat jokingly, "with good parents, nice clothing, a warm bed, and all the food you can eat, and you just sit there and get FAT...er, P-H-A-T, that is." I snap my fingers and lay back to gesture a sign of coolness. That's what "phat" means, I am told.

My point is this: they need to appreciate how comfortable they are in their every day life, while there are kids their age, suffering unbearable circumstances – not just in India, Iraq or New Orleans, but right here in their own backyard, bed-ridden and in wheelchairs, for the rest of their lives.

Chapter Fourteen

Put Words into Action

For twenty years, since 1979, I was heavily involved with a world-wide service organization, Kiwanis International, in "helping the needy throughout the world". On the local level, I was President of the Santa Ana Club in 1995 and chosen Lieutenant Governor over Division Four in 1997. I oversaw the welfare and the progress of 12 clubs throughout Orange County. I even created two new ones – one in Westminster, and another in Anaheim Hills.

Eight years ago, with the support of that Anaheim Hills Kiwanis Club, I initiated the El Rancho Builder's Club, the equivalent of the Key Club in high school.

It is all about helping others who are less fortunate than we – financially, physically, mentally, emotionally and spiritually.

Every year, our student-members do their best to "soothe" the pain of the less fortunate. They give of their money, of their time and of their skills…to help, even if it's for a little while. The Builder's Club has given to families of fallen soldiers and policemen, to leukemia and cancer patients, to the homeless of natural disasters, and to victims of gang-related shootings. Our members have taken wheel-chaired paraplegics and autistic kids bowling and fishing, and have taken food and household goods to Ronald McDonald House, a "free room and board" facility for families of (usually) terminally ill children.

I came to know the Sullivan Family through one of the members of the Builder's Club at El Rancho. In fact, the whole Anaheim Hills Community knew of the two younger siblings, Grant and Trent. At first sight you would not know that Trent was born with a severe heart ailment and had had several open heart operations, even before the age of seven. He now must be ten or eleven. He has his good days and his bad. He often comes to visit me in the classroom (that's where the candy is) and I often see him at soccer games of his older siblings.

Grant, on the other hand, was born with neuroblastoma (a form of cancer). He also visited me with his brother, whenever he could. However, he was often very sick with effects of chemotherapy and blood transfusions. At the age of seven, Grant went to be with the Lord. God took him finally to stop the suffering of this "little angel".

I took time off from teaching to be at the funeral services. The Church was packed and overflowing with people, young and old. It seemed the whole community came to honor the memory of this "gift from heaven", the boy that touched the heart of everyone he met in his brief life here on Earth.

Grant may be gone but he shall not be forgotten. In order to keep his memory alive, and to help other leukemia and cancer patients achieve their wishes, the courageous Sullivan Family has spearheaded an ongoing fundraiser in his name, GRANTS WISHES. Any donations for this worthwhile cause can be made through GRANTSWISHES.org and GRANTSWHISHES.com. God bless the Sullivans for their fortitude and benevolence.

Our Builder's Club members have even collected money and clothing for El Rancho students whose homes have burnt down. That has happened twice in the last five years. Our club members are always alert and aware of needy people and they bring that need to the attention of the Board to see if we can help. To my knowledge, we haven't turned down a single request. We have a wonderful community of volunteers and givers right here in Anaheim Hills. And you thought school was just for *readin', 'ritin', and 'rithmatic...*

Chapter Fifteen

Teach, Don't Cheat

My Spanish and French textbooks are not all that comprehensive. Therefore, it takes a knowledgeable and skillful teacher to explain and expound on what little is written on a page. That's the difference between a good instructor and a mediocre one. In college, I studied my subjects intensely, incorporating phonetics and linguistics, to learn all I can in origins of sounds and words, so that I can paint a complete picture for my students, rather than teach just rote memorization.

For example, my students know why, where, and how a word is accented. Memorization becomes long-term when one applies an association to the word. Retention is greater with an explanation of the origin of words. I couldn't teach it any other way. I'm paid to teach what I know, designed to the level of understanding of my 7th and 8th graders, of course. Anything less is cheating and stealing.

There are quite a few teachers out there who teach the same routine for 25 years – same instructions, tests, and boring classes. They'd do a great service to their students and the community to quit or retire. Thank God for the many, many others who take their jobs seriously and teach to their maximum potential. These are the kind we have here at El Rancho – just to mention a few – old timers, such as Messrs. Bower, Pitts, Sevier, and Walter, all of whom the El Rancho students adore. Likewise, there are a few new comers, such as Mrs. Porter and a new "kid" on the block, Mr. Evans. *They teach with passion.* They truly show interest *in* and care *for* their students. It shows in their students. Kids are straightforward. They tell it as they see it; they can't be fooled. They hold no punches; they'll say it to your face.

On a very sad note, our beloved Art teacher, Mr. Bob Walter, passed away last night after a long bout with cancer. Throughout his ordeal, he *never* complained. Instead, he would build *us* up. And if he wasn't bed-ridden, he was in class teaching. We extend our deepest sympathy to Joy, his wife (a fellow teacher) and his three daughters. My wife and I had the pleasure of traveling to Europe with the Walter family. It was memorable, especially the Greek Islands. Upon returning, Mr. Walter presented me with a large, hand drawing of the Eiffel Tower that hangs in my classroom. As we speak, I *know* that he's in a very special place with no more pain and suffering. *May God rest his soul.*

I learned a long time ago not to be a hypocrite. It'll catch up to you, sooner or later. I've learned to be honest and consistent with my students, unwavering – not wishy-washy – and truthful. The kids will respect a teacher *more* when that teacher is straightforward, and at the same time, compassionate. Kids need a break every so often. They need to be forgiven. Didn't we at their age? Didn't we ask for a second chance when we made bad choices?

They don't mind discipline and subsequent consequences for their errors, as long as "the punishment fits the crime". Students need to know when they've stepped out of line. They'll respect a teacher that takes appropriate action, *more* than one that ignores the situation. They want to learn. That's why they're in school – to learn. To learn good from bad, right from wrong. Most all children are good human beings. All they need is a little guidance at home, in school, at church, on a soccer field, etc....

Oh, soccer. Forgive me, but I must digress a moment, once more. To say that soccer is my life is an understatement. I drink, eat, sleep and breathe soccer, the most popular sport in the whole wide world. On June 9th, 2006, two billion (with a "b") *aficionados* (fans) will be drawn to their TV sets, while 100's of thousands will be in German stadiums, mesmerized by the football skills of Beckham, Henry, Ballack, Ronaldinho, Zidane, et al. For one solid month, the national teams of 32 countries will wage "war" against one another until one team emerges victorious, and wins the World Cup. Heavy favorites are Brazil, Germany, and France, with dark horses, Italy, England and (a long shot) the U. S. I'll come back to soccer shortly to give you results of this month-long tournament. But now, let's get back to my first love – teaching kids.

Chapter Sixteen

What's the Problem Nowadays?

Nowadays, many children in school are labeled too quickly, and erroneously, I might add. I'm not a doctor, but I'm going to go on a limb here and say that too many students are diagnosed as AD or ADHD too quickly, for the convenience of parents and/or at the whim of the psychologist. Forty years ago, there were no psychiatrists in schools and there were very few behavioral problems with students. The hyper ones were handled by the teachers, administrators and parents, working together for the common good of the child. If back then, every child that misbehaved was labeled AD, we'd have very few "normal" students in school.

Kids will be kids – hyper, slow, daydreaming, inattentive, mischievous, and the like. I'll go on another limb and say that, nowadays, the problem stems from home. We really need to train the parents. They show too many poor parental skills. Add to that the part that we feed our kids too much junk food and allow them to watch too much violence on TV, unattended. Too little exercise. It isn't surprising that our children aren't happy, healthy and well behaved. Maybe better parenting skills, better nutrition, less television and video games, more exercise and most important, teaching of morals rather than more psychiatric sessions and drugs, is the answer. Before you get really angry with me, I didn't make up these words. They are the very thoughts in a 30-year educator's letter to the editor of a local newspaper. But I couldn't have said it better myself.

As I mentioned before, kids do the "darndest" things! Yes, they don't pay attention, at times. They pass around useless notes, draw pictures, and write obscene words and pictures in classroom textbooks – all during class time. Oh yeah, text messaging is the big thing now. Aren't you glad you got your little one that all-purpose cell phone she *really* needed?

School policy states that a cell phone must not be seen nor heard in a classroom. "Yeah, catch me if you can, *Señor*!" My back turned or not, the text messages are running from one classroom to another. "I"m bored." "This class sucks." "What are you doing after school?" Real *important* stuff, you know. That is why a parent got the cell phone for the child, isn't it? For emergency situations. It couldn't have been peer pressure, *could* it...? Let me tell you that teachers and administrators can handle the emergencies in the school. What's the phone for?

A quick side bar here: I don't own a cell phone and I refuse to be a slave to that wireless gadget.
I refuse to be rude on supermarket lines and I

refuse to annoy other customers in restaurants. I refuse to risk my life and the lives of others at the wheel.

"What about emergencies," you ask? Ah, like the kids. Did we *not* have emergencies, say 15 years ago? Did we *not* take care of business, then? Were there *not* phone booths on every other corner? "Inconvenient," you say. That is possibly why we Americans are on the pudgy side in the weight column. Ooh, that hurts!

What did we lack 40 years ago, *sans* cell phones? Our parents knew where we were. *We told them.* Twelve years ago, only *one* time, one of my sons was *not* where he said he would be. I grounded him for a month. It never happened again. He's 26 today and still calls to tell me where he is. It takes discipline, respect, and common sense. That's all.

What is the *problem* nowadays? FOCUS. The kids lack focus. God forbid a lesson is too long, or the teacher is boring. They want to be entertained – as they are by television, movies and video games. One thing many teachers regretfully employ is repetition of simple commands: "Be quiet, sit down, and open the textbook". These commands *must* be repeated 4-5-6 times before they're done wholly as a class. Whenever a student is confronted, the scripted answer is: "Wha'? I dunno; I wasn't paying attention." I call these, symptoms of a disease named "thirteenitis" and... "fourteenitis", at an advanced stage. But hey, these behaviors are quite common.

Teachers need to deal with them and find ways to minimize lost time in the classroom. After all, we are older, smarter and more experienced than those little rug rats, aren't we?

I have learned, however, never to assume or presume anything about the learning process of a child. Never make comments about one's difficulties or deficiencies in learning. Some kids learn slower than others – at this age and stage.

When Spanish is not their *forté*, I highlight their computer knowledge, their musical talents or their sports skills – whatever it might be.

I say, "just give the information. Build them up. However, be honest and sincere."

I'm no saint, myself. I've made my share of mistakes in arriving at certain false judgments about a student or two. As an example, I would assume that a certain student, who had done poorly in my class, would continue that way in high school. So a year or two later, I'd meet that same student by chance. He would thank me for having taught him *and* having put up with his childishness. And much to my amazement and surprise, he would inform me that he is getting A's now, in Spanish. Another's mom, at a pancake breakfast, informed me that her daughter "Katie", was going to Spain to continue Spanish for a college course. I would *never* have supposed.... I was thrilled!

Just recently, I was angry with one of my female students for misbehaving in class. As she was hurrying out the door for her next class, I chided her for not showing interest in Spanish, to which she quickly replied, "you're wrong, Mr. K. You have sparked such a love of Spanish in me that I'm going to be a Spanish teacher, just like you."

That blew me away!

Sometimes, things are not what they appear to be. I've learned just to teach and accept their learning at their rate and level. If I do my job well, I believe my students will succeed in the future. I often tell them, "in high school, you'll be older, your brain will be larger and you'll be more focused." Age does that, you know. It *does* mature most people – kids included.

Chapter Seventeen

Build Them Up, Honestly

Every so often, I tell my students how much I love this language that I teach – whether it be Spanish or French. And they see it in my presentations. I'm *always* excited, *always* moving, *always* enthusiastic, even when I'm not up to it at times. Why? *Because it's not at all about me. It's all about helping to build up their knowledge, as well as their self-esteem.* Self esteem comes from deep down within one's self. It's one's own self worth." Therefore, beware! Don't exaggerate! They can pick up on "false self esteem." Just give them the necessary tools to build their *own* self respect.

By the same token, I tell my students, "no one can make you feel bad but yourself. Don't let anyone tell you 'you can't do it' or that 'you're not good enough'...." The great Michael Jordan, I'm told, didn't make the high school basketball team initially. However, he overcame the obstacles...and the rest is history.

"Consider the source," I tell my students. "If Mom or a close friend doubts your ability, you *may* have cause to feel hurt. If it comes from others, it's usually out of jealousy." A case in point: Last year, I found "Alex" distraught and crying in my classroom after everyone had left. She was a beautiful young lady with a bubbling personality, and very popular in school. She was even modeling for an agency. "What's the problem, my dear?" I approached her. "Kids are writing filthy things about me in text books," she cried. I explained to her what jealous people do when they have no other means. "In any case, disregard the comments with a smile, forgive them, and continue in quest of your goal."

For what is a goal? Merely a dream to be attained. Set your goals. If you've had a rough life, don't dwell on the past or the negative. Quit the self-pity party. Who said life was going to be easy, or fair? Quit complaining and thank God for your blessings. You have the choice through open-mindedness and a change in attitude to pick yourself up by the bootstraps and work toward that goal. There will be obstacles along the way. Don't be afraid of failing. *Failing is like falling.* You can get back up. It's a lesson to be learned on the way toward success. Get motivated; work hard. Through hard work and good habits, nothing is impossible to attain, if you want it bad enough.

I had mentioned that our school principal, Mr. Besta, always challenges the students in his morning "Words of Wisdom" with his parting words...*The choice is yours.* So, are you up for it?

The rewards of teaching are what keep me going. Hey, let's not fool ourselves. Teaching is tough, regardless of what some people might say. "Teachers work only from 8-3 and have 3 months off from work." *Not true.* On a good night, I'm up until 11 p.m. correcting papers or planning for the next day. Since languages in middle schools are not yet standardized by the State, as English, History and Math are, I create my own tests, according to what I've taught that week. Teaching is a tough profession, especially teaching adolescents. Some are not as interested, excited or attentive as others in the same room. But It's well worth it when one or two show exceptional insight in a rather difficult concept. And I make a point of it in class. I exclaim, "wow, how did you get that?" I usually follow it up with a reward – usually candy. Oh, I know, candy (sugar) is not good for one's *heart*, but it does wonders for the *brain*.

A quick funny side bar: I often catch a student chewing gum in class, and that is not allowed in our school. "Spit it out," is my first warning. "But Mr. K," one would often say, "chewing gum is scientifically proven to help the brain function better. "I laugh, as I have it thrown out. Anyway, gum causes ugliness under desks and chairs...and is unsightly on carpets.

Most kids listen and do the right thing. I'm big on awards and rewards. Our school recognizes "Students of the Month," "Students of the Quarter," and "Students of the Year". I have this wonderful student, Charlie Skinner. He's thirteen but he has a compassionate heart...of gold. At lunch, he gives up his leisure time to befriend students that are mentally challenged. I watch him in wonderment; I gave him my Student of the Quarter Award. Besides plaques, ribbons and trophies, I make sure to acknowledge those deserving ones the following day in the classroom, in front of their peers. I make a big deal about it because it *is* a big deal. Out of 250 students, *that* month or quarter *they* excelled, and their peers should know about it. It does wonders for building their self-esteem.

Here's how I see it: it may be wrong to extract positive results by offering rewards – like the carrot before the horse (sorry about the crude analogy). However, with children, it's good to form good habits, such as learning and retention. And if they get rewarded for that, so be it. By the way, our school rewards good citizenship as well as academics. But, not all students are academically high achievers, obviously. However, I don't have much contact in teaching underachievers, or students with physical and mental deficiencies.

Let me take a minute here to tip my hat to teachers, such as our own Messrs. Lovitt and Johnson, and Mrs. McElroy, who have dedicated themselves to teaching mentally and physically challenged students – day in and day out. I must confess that *I could not do that*. I have neither the training nor the patience. *Those* are the real teachers to be admired.

I can't even handle underachievers who are

indifferent on a prolonged basis. I'm just thankful that the students who choose French and Spanish form the top 20 % of the student body, academically. That makes my job easier, for I'm dealing with kids that are bright and receptive, for the most part. Yes, one or two may "fall through the crack", as it were. But, the percentages that pass, and pass with very high marks, are astronomical.

I can honestly say that over the last ten years, I've had no more than 3 or 4 (out of 2500 students) fail Spanish... and not even *one*, in French. Believe me, those who have failed, failed because neither *they* nor their *parents* showed any interest whatsoever throughout the year – even after my constant urging to study and retake failed tests. I've even physically fallen to my knees...pleading. *I have no pride.*

Our regular class sizes are quite large, and personal and individual attention is quite difficult. So as a rule, I come to school an hour early, stay in my room at recess and leave an hour late after school, just to give my students the opportunity to come in and learn, one-on-one.

A propos, here's a related story. Just a few years ago, I had a student that was in danger of failing my Spanish class. Throughout the year, I called his mom, wrote letters home, sent progress reports and end of quarter report cards, *and* made myself available before and after school – to no avail. No response! On the exact day of 8th Grade Promotion (the last day of school), an hour before the ceremony, the "father" and the student walked into my classroom. "Mr. Keuilian," said the man, "how are we going to pass my son who's failing your class?" To my blank stare, he continued, "what can we do to remove the "F" from his record?" (*We...? What*, you got a mouse in your pocket?) I couldn't help but laugh out loud. I wouldn't verbally insult the man, even though I wanted *so* much to say, "where were you for the last six months of your son's life...?"

I kindly showed him to the door and down the hall to the administration office. It was too late; I had already submitted the grades. This *one* time, "Daddy" couldn't solve the problem for little Johnny... at least not with *me*.

I don't want to seem indifferent or cold-hearted toward students that are in danger of failing. As a matter of fact, this week and next, I have opted to postpone my vacation and teach an intersession class to students who failed History. Without it, they would not be able to move on to next year. I love History. Furthermore, I want the challenge of teaching students who are "left behind". I believe that I can touch their hearts and minds (within that short a time), change their bad habits of learning and set them back on the road to success – as I do with my regular students. Every other semester I have done this. Quite often, in previous years, I have had students approach me to show their appreciation for the brief time we had spent together, in learning about History...and life.

Ah, the rewards of teaching....

Chapter Eighteen

El Rancho and Beyond

My students' successes do not stop with two years at El Rancho with me. I'm interested in their welfare *way* beyond their middle school years. Just the other day, as I was driving home after school, I stopped at Canyon High School (to which most of our students promote), and watched a few of my former students play intramural softball. It's not unusual for me to visit other students playing basketball, football, soccer or water polo. They get such a kick out of seeing me in the stands. They realize that I meant what I said to them a year or two previously, in that I *really* cared for them.

We all say that but soon forget, as other students fill their seats year in, year out. *Not me.* As time permits, I visit them, as they visit me. I do it not only for them but also for me. I'm a sports fanatic. I enjoy all high school sports, especially when I'm acquainted with the participants.

Just recently, I attended Canyon High School's Senior Class Graduating Ceremony, under the hot, sweltering sun. Afterwards, as I walked through the throng of graduates and their families, I was recognized by many of my former students, with whom I took pictures. They were thrilled to see me there, true to my promise.

I often call my former students on the phone to wish them a "Happy Birthday". They can't believe that I remembered their birth date. It makes their day.

Today is July the Fourth, our Independence Day. I just returned from the Annual Anaheim Hills Firecracker 5K/10K Run. There had to be over two thousand participants – moms, dads, tots, and of course, hundreds of my previous students. *It was a big party!* We got to talking. A few I had not seen in years. Many are in the best colleges throughout the country, *and* abroad. The younger ones are doing well at Canyon and other surrounding high schools.

Yes, I ran the 5K and finished in good fashion. I have witnesses. I beat out many an eighty year old, but those 10-14 year olds buzzed by me like the Roadrunner. *Oh my aching feet....*

I'd like to mention that I'm an accomplished soccer referee. And often, during high school soccer season, I officiate a few of their games, either at their home school field or away. Even in the summer off-season, at first sight, they run up to hug and give high fives. It happens so every often, and it happened just yesterday with Courtney H. and Linzey S. in a San Juan Capistrano tournament. I advise them not to, so as not to show favoritism in the eyes of their opponents. *It's such a kick!*

As I mentioned, throughout the year, and not at any special occasion, there will be many, many ex-students who come back to visit. They may be high school freshmen or college graduates. Just this afternoon, during French class, there walked in Sajeda Kermally, one of the brightest French students of my ten years at El Rancho. I had not seen her in eight years. Impromptu, she mentioned to the class what an inspiration I had been to her in her educational drive and success. She graduated John Hopkins University and now is in her second year of pre-med in Canada.

The mother of another beautiful young lady who also took French some years back, Kelsey Warren, stopped me in the parking lot of Von's Supermarket just the other day to inform me that Kelsey is continuing French at Marquette University and "she wanted Mr. K. to know about it". I ran into Kelsey a few months back at San Antonio's Fair and she was extremely excited about her future. I hope she's also continuing Drama. I have attended two of her performances at Canyon High School plays and she's an accomplished actress to boot.

You want to hear another one? During our three week Fall break, I'm in my classroom cleaning, one random day. The door is open behind me. And who walks in out of the blue? Michelle Guerrero, one of my year-2000 grads. Her hair is still as curly as ever. She looks just a little older and prettier than six years ago. She's in her second year at Cal State

University at Fullerton.

Here's one more for good measure. Prior to attending a musical, performed by many of my students at our school last month, I ran into another one of my former students, Chris Emami, who had been at my classroom door waiting to see me. To make a long story short, this student, who was carefree at the age of thirteen (1997), has turned out to be a responsible citizen who is actually running for a Board position in our own Orange Unified School District. I wish him the best of luck.

Here is the last, but not the least. This morning, as I was about to begin teaching my first period Spanish class, there walks in this good-looking, muscle-bound U.S. Serviceman in gear (camouflage). I immediately recognized the face but the name escaped me. After all, it had been seven years since Lance Corporal Anthony Stout was taking first-year French in my class. I invited him to speak to my students and he did, so eloquently. He had very nice words to say about me as his role model. He also spoke emphatically about the value of a good education.

I thanked him for his service to protect our country and told him in front of all my students how much I loved him. I gave him a great, big hug.

Unbelievable! What a thrill to know that I've made a positive impact on those who take the time to return and tell me about their achievements in life!

Ah, the rewards of teaching....

Hey, I'm getting on in my years. I'll be sixty in

October; I won't be teaching forever. My energy level is slowly dwindling. Most days, after school, I get home and "crash" on the couch for an hour. I'm *drained.* During the day, I've given all I had. And it takes its toll on me. Ask my Pastor, I can't even stay awake in church on Sundays.

On many occasions, colleagues of mine, who have observed me over the years, tell me to slow down or "you'll burn out". They don't really comprehend that my strength doesn't come from me. If it did, I'd be "gone" by now.

I thank the Lord for keeping me healthy and sane, so that I can accomplish *His* will. What is *that*?

To be able to touch the minds and hearts of each and every student with whom I'm in contact.

Usually, they are students from my classes. However, there are times when other students in the school approach me with their personal problems. That blows me away. That's not because of *me*. That is *God's* work. There's not a day that goes by that I don't get numerous hugs and high fives... an occasional "I love you, Mr. K". I *teach* my students about love, and *that* love spreads throughout the campus. Love is contagious. We all need it to survive.

How could I explain this phenomenon? I can honestly tell you that in my ten years at El Rancho, I have *never* met a student I didn't like. I may not like what they *do*. But I cherish them all; they're God's own creation. *To me, they're all precious.* And this age group of 12-14 year olds is unique. They are exciting to teach and to mold. They are *so* impressionable; and I only have two years to form some good, decent values in them. Also, within those two years, I have an opportunity to open their minds and hearts to a language about which they know very little. Whether it's Spanish or French, they are apprehensive – at times, downright terrified. It's my responsibility to ease their minds and get them readily interested.

The first day of the school year is critical for me. First impressions, you know. To make sure I actually show my passion for the language, I put on a show. Did I tell you that I'm a frustrated actor? Aren't *all* teachers? In my case, I really am. I've acted in plays all my life, and throughout my high school and college years. Even in Church and community plays. *I play a mean Scrooge.* I've always wanted to be an actor. Anyway, here's my chance. No fakery, just a good, clean, fun show – winning the audience over, so to speak.

I take my job quite seriously. After all, these are kids that I'm dealing with: impressionable, naïve, and inexperienced. As I win their confidence, I take on even more of a responsibility to do my utmost not to err in my ways. They look up to me, trust me and open up to me. *And they do.* They come to me with many problems – peer, school and at times, personal. I'm old enough to know what to say or do. In my ten years at El Rancho, I've met a few students with serious problems. Teachers need to be alert to detect, solve or direct (to the counselors) such problems in students. I'm a father of two boys (and grandfather of one little girl). My own boys had gone through the same exact problems facing my students today. I handled those. As a matter of fact, I remember my *own* junior high school years, with similar problems. *We all survive...I assure them of that.*

Chapter Nineteen

Different but Equal

As I've mentioned before, our school has quite diverse demographics. At last count, it is mainly split three ways, predominantly Whites, Far East Asians and Middle Easterners, respectively. Of course, almost all the students are American-born and mostly Southern Californians.

I want to state up front that I have no specific favorites, even though I am a Middle Easterner by birth.

I *do* want to say, however, that the Middle Eastern students – Arabic, Iraqi and Iranian – tend to be more family oriented and warmer people. That's because of their grandparents and parents. It's totally a different culture than the American.

As an example, in Anaheim Hills (where I live and teach), the main difference between the American family and its foreign counterpart is the bond and unity of its members – generally speaking.

Just the facts: American born parents' divorce rate is astronomical. There are too many broken families, multiple parents, stepmothers and fathers, step brothers and sisters, foster parents and children, etc.

And it breaks my heart to see the little ones get caught in the middle....

You will seldom find this situation in the Middle and Far Eastern cultures. They have solid, two-parent families. Their children consequently thrive on that close-knit family atmosphere. They also thrive in education and moral values.

Speaking of differences in culture, I hope all teachers are aware that when they're disciplining a foreign student, they should expect different responses. Do not demand that a child look you in the eyes and "knock off that smirk". First of all, it is not a smirk; it's a sign of shamefulness or timidity. Secondly, foreign kids do not look directly at adults – out of respect. This goes for Far Eastern kids, as well as Hispanics. I trust that most teachers remember these behavioral differences from their teaching credential classes. Nevertheless, it is common sense that there *are* differences, and teachers and administrators *should be* aware.

However, you won't find many foreign students getting into trouble in school anyway.

I myself come from a family where Mom and Dad were married for 55 years, until their demise. My own marriage will reach 40 years come next July. I've been happily married to the same woman for 25 years. We simply don't believe in divorce. *Murder yes, divorce, no.* Sorry for the tasteless jokes. Seriously though, marriage tends to last longer, much longer in Asian families than that of Americans. It's a fact. Now, whether the longer marriages are happier ones, I can only speak from my own experiences. My brothers and sister are also married for 40 years and over, respectively.

Before I make too many enemies, I want to say that I have met many, many beautiful, warm and caring American parents.

I know this may be opening a can of worms but I *must* mention at least two beautiful American families whose three siblings (daughters) I've had as students from each respective family: the Bush (Lauren, Megan and Shannon) and the Hoffman (Sarah, Stacey and Sabrina) Families. I've *got* to mention two others: the Tait (Whitney, Trevor and Kendall) and the Chapman (Kristin, Nicole and Karissa) Families. I would be remiss if I did not mention the Barr brothers (Matt, Andy and Stephen).

They've *all* been a delight to teach. I have been blessed and honored to have them in my life, even for the brief two years each. *Truly outstanding and respectful students.* An apple does not fall far from the tree. And there are so many more....

I'm just stating facts as I see them. Ten years is a long enough time, in one area, to form an educated opinion of the population.

Let me stick to the point of raising kids in such

an environment and circumstance. In general, the children of American parents do not "open up" and *show* love and respect as readily as the Eurasians. It takes them much longer to solidify trust and friendship with a teacher, such as myself. And that is OK. I truly know firsthand why that's so. Some come from broken families and some come from single parent backgrounds, where trusting an adult, albeit a teacher, becomes difficult. That is not to say that these kids have different emotions as their counterparts. The feelings are there; they just take a little longer to express.

Here's something that may sound contradictory: Most of the kids in my school that greet me with "I Love You, Mr. K" are pure American kids.

Isn't that something?

Let me try to explain this phenomenon. I hope you'll understand. It took me a while to figure it out myself. Most Asian students have a hard time telling a teacher they love him. They truly *respect* him. But because of their upbringing, they think that showing outward affection towards anyone other than parents and relatives is discourteous, according to their culture.

On the other hand, American kids are free of such restraints. They say what they feel. *I love that!* It's a cultural thing. The teen years of children of the Easterners are quite difficult, trying to juggle two different cultures – their parents' and that of their classmates. They mimic one in school and live another at home.

Hey, children of *all* backgrounds have a difficult go of life. That's part of growing up. However, the Middle Eastern kids seem to identify readily with me. Ask Cathy T., Sheila G., Lilya R., Sina P., Sheila S., Rayan N., and Nicole H. if that isn't true. I even *look like* their fathers and grandfathers.

In features, I'm tall, dark and handsome. Well, I'm at least...dark and handsome. Two out of three *"ain't"* bad. Seriously, our features and our languages are similar. Our foods are alike. Our history is akin. Honestly, in my ten years teaching these Middle Eastern kids, I've been told, "Mr. Keuilian, you talk and act just like my father/grandfather, the things you say, the stories you tell, your mannerisms..." I guess that's an ultimate compliment. That is why there's great love and closeness among us. We're from the same area, with similar cultures. Why should it be any different?

I must add also that because of my features and characteristics, I also resemble Hispanic fathers, such as those of Megan and Chelsea L., Sergio and David A., Patty and Gabby C. and Nelly and Jessica A.

During Parent Night (I may have told you this, but it's worth repeating), I open up my heart to *all* parents and genuinely ask for their confidence and faith in me. I ask them to trust me in teaching, admonishing, disciplining and protecting their children while in my care – as *they* do at home. 99.9% of parents give me their vote of confidence, for they believe that I *am* an extension of themselves in school.

And I would *never* break that trust. Kidding, some request that I use whatever means necessary to "guide" their children along, if you know what I mean.

I don't believe in physical punishment of students, even though I received some in my elementary and secondary education, back in Jordan *and* in New York.

And it did me "good."

God forbid, parents found out that their child was "scolded" or "paddled" by a teacher in school that day. *No questions asked.* That night, that child would get another beating at home for having disrespected the teacher. Try that scenario in our schools *these* days. Parents would be at the Principal's Office at the crack of dawn, possibly accompanied by an attorney and/or the police. Well, maybe not to that extreme. But you get the picture, don't you?

Chapter Twenty

It's a Cultural (Religious) Thing

In my classroom, I try to dismiss certain cultural differences, while at the same time, note and emphasize certain special events. We celebrate all birthdays, bar and bat mitzvahs, Ramadan, Rosh Hashanah, Cinco de mayo, and Persian, Indian, Chinese and Vietnamese New Year. We also celebrate Christmas, which has become a hot topic lately. It's funny how the traditional Christmas and Easter vacations are now called Winter and Spring Breaks, respectively. Dates haven't changed; just names.

I'm not angry, even though I *am* Christian. I'm just stating facts, much like... should we keep saying ..."under God..." in our Pledge of Allegiance, just because we've been doing it for over a half a century? I *am* being sarcastic, of course.

I'm Christian, and in my classes, I have Jews, Muslims, Hindus, Buddhists, Mormons, Jehovah Witnesses... and even an occasional atheist. I honestly respect them all. Well, almost all. I do not preach Christianity in the classroom. That would be against the law. However, I *do often* teach Christian principals of love, honor, respect, compassion and other virtues – similar to all other beliefs, except atheism. I don't care much for that, but I don't make my feelings known. When a child, at thirteen, tells me that he does not believe in a higher Being, then I know that a parent is talking. That's fine. Parents are ultimately responsible for their young ones. I pray, however, that one day that child will "grow" to choose for himself – without the influence of the parent.

Sorry to digress. Religion and politics are two, too volatile subjects to discuss. Thank God that in the United States we *can*, without repercussions. That is what is unique about America. Why did our forefathers leave England...?

Let me for one moment confide in you, off the record. Why is it that our History text books write about Buddha, Mohammed, Joseph Smith and other deities and "prophets", but very little about God and Jesus Christ? Why is it that people can use God's name, as in "God dammit"...or Jesus', as in "Jesus freaking Christ" and it seems harmless and accepted? However, try using God and His Son as examples of goodness and love, and people get bent out of shape. Which one would you choose in teaching your child...?

I'm sorry, Lord. Forgive me for using Your Name in vain, even as an example.

Chapter Twenty One

Love, Love, Love

Let's talk about love for a moment (as if I haven't already). *I'm big on love.* I mentioned that I never met a student that I did not like. But I'm talking about love, God's Agape love. I tell *all* my students that I love them, daily – girl, boy, bright, not so bright, good, not so.... It does not matter. The Lord has created them all equal, yet unique, in their own way. I tell them *that* also. I emphasize their strengths and minimize their weaknesses in front of their peers. It's amazing how opportunities arise, while teaching, to talk to them about life and love.

Last week, I was teaching the class a Spanish song called *Cielito Lindo,* loosely translated as "My Little Heaven". More like, "my little darling", a nickname a loving parent may have for his child. "Who has a cute nickname at home?" I asked, catching them off guard. No one answered. Kids this age feel embarrassed to reveal such intimate details of their lives. And that's fine. I've taught them not to tell family secrets to anyone – not even to their best friends. But this lesson was about the Spanish suffix *"ito/ita"*, a diminutive, which added to a noun, makes the item small and lovable. For example, *un gatito* is a lovable, little pussycat. *Una abuelita* is a cuddly, little grandma. A small taco is a *taquito*. A small judge is a *Judge Ito*. Remember? Ooh, such a bad joke! To get back on track, then, *cielito* is an adorable little child, in this instance.

To break the ice, I volunteered, "my father used to call me *"Mum"*. They all laughed out loud. I explained that it's an Armenian diminutive for Mom...mommy. "Yes," I confirmed, "he loved my Mom *so much* that he shared her name with me and my twin sister.

I remember him calling me that all my life, up to his death. He passed away at 73. I was 40, married, with children. "Guess what?" I continued. "Guess what I call my sons *even* to this day?"..."*Hyrig*" "daddy" in Armenian. Yeah, I have the same love for my kids as I had for my Dad. Once they heard that, they volunteered with "Coco Puffs", "Sweetie Pie", "Snuggem", etc. All I wanted to do was allow them to express themselves and not to be ashamed to show love. "Love is the greatest of them all..." the Bible says.

It seems difficult for American kids to talk of love...or the lack thereof, even within the family. I understand. When there *is* much love within their own family, their peers may not appreciate their expressing it, probably lacking that in their own home. Or possibly, they misunderstand the connotation of love. They do not want to talk about it or show it in public. Especially boys.

Our American society looks down upon "manly love", in its true sense. Do you know that my two sons, now in their upper-twenties, kiss me (on the lips), during hello and goodbye? In their junior and high school years, they were never ashamed, even in front of their American friends, to show affection toward their parents. It's an Armenian custom. It "shows" love for one another. *Oh, if we only had that throughout....*

In my classroom, I have a poster that shows how love can solve almost any problem a child may encounter. It's good for adults too. It's both in English and Spanish. Also in my classroom, I have a collage of photographs of present and previous students, in the shape of a humongous heart – for *all* to see.

I have honestly broken through to my students with the message of love. You would never have caught a boy showing signs of love in a classroom setting. Here's another true story to that effect. "Michael" was a tough cookie to crack earlier this year. Quite mischievous. He showed little interest for Spanish and even less respect for me and his classmates. He was very disruptive, to say the least. Many of his teachers complained about his behavior in their classes as well. Rather than hand him referrals, I showed him kindness, understanding, patience and love. In short, there's not a day that goes by that he doesn't greet me with, "I love you, Mr. K". *This is a fourteen year old boy.*

On the other hand, with girls, it comes a bit easier to show affection. However, I don't easily buy it. I tell them, "show me deeds, not words. At home you say, 'Mommy, I love you,' but you won't take out the garbage, do your homework, or clear the table...What kind of love is that? Same in the classroom. While I'm teaching, you talk, write useless notes, and chew gum. And you say you love me? *'What's **love** got to do with it?'* "

Their excuses won't cut it with me either. In my classes parents must weekly sign off a test taken by the student – to show that they are aware of their child's progress. The kids always have an excuse for not having done it. I tell them, "your best excuse *plus* a $1.75 will buy you the best cup of coffee and a donut at *Dee's Donuts...*"

Speaking of excuses, here is a partial list for *not* having done homework:

1. My dog chewed up my homework (yep, we *still* get this one).

2. I forgot it in my mother's car. You can call her...

2. I did it but can't find it. My mother *saw* me do it. Ask her....

4. I left it at my dad's house in Van Nuys – really!

Call him if you don't believe me.

5. Yes, that's my mom's signature. She signs that way. She's always in a hurry.

6. I showed her the test but I forgot to have her sign it.

7. My little brother ripped it up and threw it away. Honest.

8. You're not going to believe this, Mr. K, but....

9. My parents are on vacation for a week and I'm *all* alone....

10. Wasn't that homework due *next* week? I *swear* I heard you say that!

I have my own comebacks that go like this:

1. Please don't take me for a fool. I was born at night but it wasn't *last* night.

2. Hey, don't pull that on me. I didn't just fall off a turnip truck.

3. It's not that I don't believe you, I just... don't believe you.

4. That excuse plus a $1.75 will buy you the best cup of coffee....

5. No excuses please, just results.

6. Keep that up and you'll end up at an off ramp, with a sign: "Will work for food."

7. Let me write that excuse down; I don't think I've heard *that* before.

8. Can't you come up with something better than that?

9. If you're going to lie, why don't you embellish it a bit more?

10. You can be a little more creative, can't you?

I had mentioned previously that the "outbursts of love" occur even in the middle of instruction – at random. Other times, it's outside of the class, during nutrition or lunch break. There's not a moment when a student doesn't rush up with open arms – in front of other teachers or students. *Even students who don't take my classes show the "love".* We form bonds on campus. Word gets around. I can't fully explain this phenomenon.

I know one thing. *It's got to be God's love they see in me, that's all.*

And all this love is in an environment where such overt expressions are almost taboo.

Why? Why should it be that way?

As I mentioned before, we live in a time where our young people are preyed upon constantly, by adults. Whom should they trust? The situation worsens when the violators are teachers. Teachers are supposed to be trustworthy and moral individuals. Parents send their children to school to a safe environment, where the students can learn and grow without fear and apprehension.

Chapter Twenty Two

Touch the Heart

Very often, we send mixed messages to our children and students. Parents teach their kids to be respectful and courteous to others. So do teachers. And yet, we also tell them to beware of others and be cautious. Stay away. Nevertheless, over the PA system, the counselors advise the students to smile, be kind, and hug someone to make their day. Forget the students for a moment. *I'm confused.*

Teachers often tell each other to stay clear of the kids for fear of lawsuits. It's a legitimate fear. It happens all too often that a student falsely accuses a teacher of wrongdoing – to get even. What are we to *do*?

After all that, would I recommend that other teachers get close to their students? I advise many a young colleague to use discretion.

In fact, I have suggested that they do not touch. However, it has a lot to do with the character and the personality of each individual teacher. What seems appropriate for one may not seem so for another.

In my case, I don't initiate touching, and I touch no one alone. It's always in open places and always with other students, teachers or parents present. When a student walks into my room alone, I *always* keep the door wide open. Hey, I'm neither naïve nor stupid. I mentioned a moment ago that I am aware of students' fantasies and even lies, to get back at a teacher. I understand what perceptions others may have. However, that is *not* going to change my character and personality. *I am what I am.*

Here's a pure coincidence. Two Sundays ago at church, I picked up a flier at the ministry's table. It listed *8 Touches to a Teen Heart* by Shelly Roberts, my Pastor's wife and Youth Director. It goes something like this:

1. Be a Willing Listener–During the adolescent years, teens can become confused about their identity and the world around them. Be a safe place for them to work out their conflict.

2. Give Them Praise–Praise will build a positive self-image in teens as well as strengthen their personal character.

3. Show Positive Affection–Teens need the warm feeling of belonging that come from good touches and hugs.

4. Offer Straightforward Feedback–When it comes to

important issues like drugs, sex and drinking, teens want straightforward guidance. But don't nag.

5. Be Available–Teens often want to talk about things at the most unusual moments. Take time to interact with them during these times. It will validate their importance to you.

6. Keep Calm–When dealing with teens, there are times where they may become critical or harsh. Do not take it personally. Help them work through these times, teaching them to express themselves properly.

7. Laugh Together–Laughter is good medicine.

8. Present Unconditional Love–It is important that teens feel unconditional love, especially when they feel that they have failed you or themselves.

Why can't I write such words of wisdom? I know Mrs. Roberts will not mind my using them. But I know it will cost me at least 10%, if you know what I mean.

At the beginning of each school year, I assure all parents present at "Open House" that their children will be protected from any harm while in my care. The parents have my word, an oath I've made to them *and* to God. It's not uncommon that I am called to stop a fight between students, console a grieving child, or even defend a "wronged" student by a teacher or counselor. I take my job very seriously when it comes to the children. Their parents and they depend on me. Because of that, I'm quite vigilant. My classroom overlooks the front campus and the parking lot. I chose that room so that I can keep an eye on *all* students (and adults) that come and go. Between classes, I "hang" outside my door looking for troublemakers, as hundreds of students rush by to their next class. I stop many a skirmish, horsing around, bullying and harassment.

I also catch numerous high fives and an occasional "I love you, Mr. K". I always have a smile on my face and a song on my lips. Sometimes, I put on my *poncho* and *sombrero*, and I sing *en español*. Other times, I don a cowboy hat and wail a country ballad. I "hurry along" students who think they're on a Sunday promenade. And I slow down those who think they're on a race track. It's part of my teaching process. As I promised their parents, I'm creating a safe and fun climate. Oftentimes, kids do mischief without realizing the immediate consequences of their actions. I'm there to eliminate the danger *before* it presents itself.

Almost every year, the administration asks me to move my classroom to the back of the campus, away from other classrooms. This year was no exception. There have been complaints about my teaching too loudly, disturbing other teachers. All right, so I'm loud. There's a good reason for that: *I'm Armenian.* We're just boisterous. In my case, I love my classes so much that I lose myself in my teaching. *I'm not pulling your leg.* I teach with excitement, and I wear my passion on my sleeves, so to speak. Okay, I wear it on my tongue. This seems to disturb the teachers on either side of me. One reason is that the walls between us are roll-away-type-heavy-cardboard plaster. What do you expect?

Anyway, I have refused to move, year after year. Year in and year out, the teachers around me have moved, until recently. For the last two years I've had a male teacher on either side of me. We *all* get along; we *all* make noise, within reason. And it's working well. However, nothing good lasts forever. The gentleman on my right has decided to retire. *Well, that's life!* But I'm not giving up nor giving in. I'm praying for a well-seasoned, understanding, and *rambunctious* teacher, just like me, to take his classroom.

Chapter Twenty Three

"GOOOOL"
Soccer Is My Life

As I promised, I'll tell you more about soccer and my life – which could be synonymous. Some weekdays and *all* Saturdays are dedicated to this most beautiful sport. Just running on a grassy field – at times over 5 hours, intermittently – gives me the greatest high. Who needs drugs? A few hours on the field give me peace and sanity – an escape from the pressures of life – no doctor can prescribe. Who needs a shrink? The exercise keeps me healthy and in good shape. It's the best activity for kids. Soccer teaches discipline, skills, camaraderie, team-work, patience, humility – you name it. *Ah, the thrill of victory...and the agony of defeat!*

I've been playing soccer all my life – ever since I can remember. I have played through kindergarten, elementary, middle and high school, and college – and even to the ripe old age of 59. I have recently slowed down a bit, having torn ligaments in my knee.

Soccer players don't die; they just fade away.

I have coached my two boys in soccer from age six through high school. Before my kids were born, I coached college kids in summer league, winning every trophy imaginable. *I was a good coach if I may say so myself.* I've made a lot of good friends, young men who have become husbands and fathers in their own right... and excellent coaches.

Lately, however, I've leaned heavily toward refereeing the game, something I've done for the last 24 years. "If you can't fight them, join them," I always say. Seriously, I enjoy refereeing youth games immensely. Youth soccer is very popular in the United States. In fact, many of my students (Taylor M., Courtney H., Serenity S., Ashley C., Adrian F., Jenny W., Hailey J. and Brendan N. ... just to name a few) play weekly on organized teams throughout the county. I see them on fields all over Southern California while I'm officiating. Many of them are also referees. Take Asal A., J.J., Eric M., Nathan L., Zack E., the Green and Talmas brothers, and many others....

In high school, it is one of the major seasonal sports, and colleges offer large scholarships for skillful prospects. Since the fifties, it has become more and more popular as a professional sport, forming leagues, such as the Major League Soccer, which competes not only within the Unites States but also throughout the world. We have world class American players who play for European powerhouses, such as Bayern

Munich of Germany and Manchester United of England. As we speak, we are at the end of the greatest extravaganza, the World Cup, being held in Germany this time.

Here's the latest and final news on the Tournament: In the semi-final, Italy knocked out Germany while France beat out Portugal. The winners battled for the coveted Cup. In the Final, Zinedine Zidane, who plays for *Les Bleus*, the French National Team, and is arguably the world's greatest soccer player of the decade, committed one of the ugliest fouls I've ever seen in all my life as a player, coach, referee and spectator. In a 1-1 tie near the end of overtime, after a brief verbal encounter with the Italian defender Materazzi, *and without warning*, Zidane viciously thrust his head into the chest of the unsuspecting opponent, caving him onto the ground.

Was it something the Italian defender said? It *is* rumored that the "victim" had made a hateful and racial remark against the Algerian/ Frenchman. Consequently, the referee sent off (red carded) the usually volatile Frenchman for the remainder of the match that eventually ended in a tie. Hence, in the ensuing penalty kicks (kicks from the penalty mark) to determine a winner, Italy made *all* their kicks into the net, while France missed *one*. That decided the winner of the 2006 World Cup-ITALY.

With one horrendous infraction, Zinadene Zidane, worshipped in France, Algeria and the rest of the world (certainly one of my favorite players), turned from being a *hero* into a *goat*. Because of his ejection, one of the best penalty shooters of the tournament (he had already scored two) could not participate in the final kicks. Thus the demise of France.

Zidane, who came out of retirement to help France qualify for the World Cup, had said that he would quit soccer completely at the end of the tournament. He could have left the game a legend, unmarred. Instead, he has left shamefully. As for Materazzi, the Italian defender, I believe justice will be "served"....

What was Zidane thinking? Or was he at all...?

One of the lessons I teach in class has to do with "Problem Solving". I have mentioned this before. And one way to have solved Zidane's dilemma was to *ignore and walk away*, especially with so much at stake. Of course, we all know the adage, "Sticks and stones may break my bones but words shall never hurt me". *Truer words were never spoken.*

Furthermore, Zidane should have considered the source and the motive of the insidious remark... besides the jealousy factor. It was to provoke a negative response or reaction. And it worked. *Zizou,* as he is affectionately called by his teammates and adoring fans, ironically won the Golden Ball Award as this World Cup's best player. *Go figure!* Unfortunately, he *is* a role model (an idol) to millions of young fans. Hopefully, something good will come out of this unfortunate incident.

Chapter Twenty Four

Hye Em Yes
I Am an Armenian

I have often mentioned that I'm an Armenian. *But who are the Armenians?* We are one of the oldest races in history, as ancient as Babylonians, Jews and Greeks. Today we number about seven million with three million in the Republic of Armenia. The rest are scattered all over the world, with a very heavy population in the United States, California in particular.

Armenia is located in Asia Minor, south of the Caucasus and the Black Sea. It is a land of mostly mountains and valleys, rivers and lakes. We belong to the Caucasian race, people of average height, mostly with black hair and dark eyes. That's why my wife fell in love with me. I'm serious...and because I was rich and good-looking, also. Generally, Armenians are God-fearing, hard-working and law-abiding people.

Armenians call themselves *Hye* (pronounced "high"). "*Hye em yes*" is a popular and proud statement which translates into *I am an Armenian.* I had mentioned that my brothers and my sons are *all* named after Armenian Kings of old. We have a long and illustrious history of kings and kingdoms.

Then came the "terrible" Turks in 1375. Armenia suffered under the yoke of the Turkish misrule for more than five centuries. At any sign of an Armenian awakening of independence, the Turks stifled all aspirations.

The trouble with our ancestors was that they often fought with a "cross" rather than a "sword" in hand.

Our enemy resorted to cruel massacres (as I mentioned before) which culminated in the shameful holocaust of 1915-1923. This has come to be known as the First Genocide of the Twentieth Century. More than two million men, women and children fell victim (almost two-thirds of the Armenian population). Furthermore, the Turks annexed more than two-thirds of Armenia to Turkey. *But no nation cared.* Later in history, in a documented story, Hitler was warned by his generals, citing the Armenian Massacre, that he would not get away with such atrocities against the Jews. And his answer was: "After all, who remembers the Armenians?" *Oh, so true.*

Armenians are mostly Christian by faith, having embraced Christianity in the year 301. The Church was founded by two disciples of Jesus, Bartholomew and Thaddeus. The language belongs to the European family of languages. It has two dialects: Eastern (spoken in Armenia, the Soviet Union and Iran), and Western (spoken in the Middle East and the Diaspora – the rest of the world). The differences are minor and we can understand each other. Armenian is written from left to right, has 38 letters in the alphabet and it's easy to learn, in that, much like Spanish, the sound of each letter never varies in pronunciation.

Armenians are highly educated people; illiteracy is virtually nonexistent. The city of Yerevan, the Capital of Armenia, has over 200 schools and 120 libraries.

I mentioned previously that Armenia was instrumental in the Crusades by bridging the East to the West. However, I did not know that in 1305, Marco Polo had made his journey to China by crossing through Armenia. Boy! That's a long way to go just for pizza.

Seriously though, I am deeply indebted to Hagop Terjimanian, whose booklet *"Who Are the Armenians?"* gave me all these tidbits to pass on to you. He also noted some meaningful Armenian proverbs I like to share with you:

1. Jealousy first hurts the jealous.

3. If you have fingernails, scratch your head (Don't depend on others).

3. Be good. If men don't see you, God will.

4. Don't pollute the well; someday you may need it.

5. A sweet word will bring the snake out of its hole.

6. Let's say O.K. so that it may be O.K.

7. What the sword cuts *heals*; what the tongue cuts *doesn't*.

8. From mouth to mouth, a splinter becomes a log.

9. Measure ten times, cut once.

10. Tell the truth in the form of a joke.

Now that you know a lot about Armenians, let me mention a few prominent ones you may recognize by name:

Kirk Kirkorian, Las Vegas Casino owner, financier and philanthropist.

George Deukmejian, former Governor of California, and attorney at law.

Ara Parseghian, former Notre Dame Football coach.

Jerry Tarkanian, former San Jose, Las Vegas and Long Beach State University basketball coach.

William Saroyan, noted American/Armenian novelist.

Rouben Mamoulian, American motion picture director.

Mike Connors, a motion picture star/actor. (Some change names for fame).

Charles Aznavour, a French singer/crooner of love songs.

André Agassi, an outstanding, famous American tennis player/star.

Cher, the late Sonny Bono's singing partner/wife, an American Diva.

Chapter Twenty Five

My Family

On a few occasions, I mentioned my two sons, Armen Jr. and Aram, and my beautiful wife, Jeannie. Permit me now to boast about them a bit, for God blessed me with a wonderful family. I don't believe I mentioned that I married an *odar*, an outsider (from my nationality). She's an Italian-American, born in the Bronx.

It was very difficult for me to break the news to my parents that I was going to wed my childhood sweetheart. If I were to marry, it would *have* to be an Armenian.... Yes, they knew that I was seeing her, but contemplating marriage? *NEVER.* After all, my older brother Ard had eloped with an *odar*, and they downright disowned him for the longest time.

"How could you do this to us?" they'd cry. *Actually cry.* My father was a staunch Armenian, having suffered so much just for *being* an Armenian. He had a saying (forgive me for the crude language), *"Hye togh ellah, kak togh ellah*-Let it be Armenian, let it be shit." That's how much he believed in perpetuating the Armenian heritage. You can imagine the speeches *not* to do such a dishonorable thing. "It would bring shame to the family. What would friends and relatives say?"

"But *hyrig,*" I'd plead, "She's *like* an Armenian, from a very respectable Italian family. She's Christian and she's pure." To no avail.

My parents would not give their blessing. However, LOVE has rights. It transcends race, color and creed, especially here in the United States. So, we got engaged secretly. I slipped a ring on her finger one night and took off to California the next morning, without her. My older brother had returned from California to move the family and furniture. I had to go. That was a cowardly thing to do on my part. I told her that if she *really* loved me, she would have to win them over, herself.

My wife is an angel. She took on the challenge. During my one year of absence from New York, she visited my parents often, learned *some* Armenian, and *lots* of Armenian cooking from my Mom. Once they got to know her, they truly loved her.

You see, the Italian culture and customs are quite similar to ours. For instance, she has very strong family values where the *father* is the head of the household – much like it says in the Bible. This arrangement produces family strength and idealism. This may shock you, but my wife Jeannie was a virtuous young lady when we were dating all those years.

And I'm proud to say that she was a virgin when I married her. And so was I.

She is a great cook and a wonderful, giving person. When we moved to California the day after we wed, she left behind all her family, relatives and friends. As with Armenians, Italians have quite an extended family of uncles, aunts and cousins. My wife gave *all that up* just for me, even though she was very close to her ailing mother. *What did she see in me?*

For the first eleven years of our marriage, we could not have children. Doctors had told us that her uterus was intertwined and she would not be able to bear a child. We tried everything and we took advice from everyone. "Stand on your head after you do it," one sister-in-law would advise. Another would suggest, "try it with one sock on, upside down, inside out, downside up...." *Enough already!* She felt incomplete, and our relationship began to suffer. I could not handle her tears every night, even when I promised that I loved *her*, even *before* any talk of babies. "In God's time..." I would reassure her.

Are you ready for a miracle? In 1977, my wife's godfather, Frank, who lived in Florida, came out to visit us in California. He and his wife, Florence, both in their late sixties, drove their motor home across country one summer and spent a few days with us. On the morning of their departure back home, right in the office of my workplace, Florence asked my wife why she had no kids. My wife explained in detail, in tears. "Why don't you ask Frank to pray over you?" she blurted. Not to be rude, we agreed. What did we have to lose? Frank laid his hand over Jeannie's stomach, prayed in silence and nonchalantly said, "you will bear a child in six months and it'll be a son." And as he walked away, he mentioned that there will also be another child, to which his wife added, "And *that* one will be a girl."

We laughed it off as we said our goodbyes, and never again paid mind. To the exact month of Frank's prophecy, one day while I was at work, my wife frantically drove into the shop, and overjoyed, shrieked with excitement, "lov, lov (she calls me lov), I'm pregnant! We're going to have a baby!" *The rabbit died.* Long story short, we had our first child that November, days before her 30th birthday. *That* was a milestone for her.

Let me not minimize the greatness of this miracle. This same Frank was the man that came to her rescue once before, when Jeannie was only two years old, in New York. At that age, she came down with severe pneumonia and was given very little chance to survive the night. Only by chance (or was it?), Frank, who had not been seen for years, showed up *that* night at the door, unannounced, and at random. He prayed over her, I am told. That very next morning, this toddler showed nary a sign of any illness.

Praise God!

Coincidence? *Nah!* As we found out later, Frank was God-sent. He was an evangelist and a healer. He had healed numerous others, even long distance – through the phone. The miracles are documented.

It's hard to believe these things (even for a believer), if it doesn't happen to you personally. But it *did* happen to us and we *did* have not only one child but also a second boy. If you were attentive, the prediction was that the second child was to be...female. Yes, we also fell for that. In fact, near the last term of her pregnancy, Jeannie began to decorate the baby's room in pink – paint, curtains, and crib.

As we called Frank to give him the good news, we asked how he was mistaken on *that* particular point. "You may recall," He chided us, "I had said, '...another child.' It was Florence, my wife, who put her two cents in about the gender of that child." As we look back, he was absolutely correct.

Since we were so sure to have a baby girl for our second child, my wife had already picked out the name, Jennifer. We had no back-up boy's name. Who needed it? Luckily, by chance, I was reading a book at the hospital, during my wife's 24 hour labor ordeal. It was called *My Name is Aram*, by William Saroyan. Therefore, on the spur of the moment, while my wife was still in delirium, I slipped the nurse the child's name, Aram. And so it was, in honor of another ancient Armenian king. These are true stories, so help me....

Our boys were born in the city of Huntington

Beach about two and a half years apart. They were very close companions in their early years, all the way up to middle school. Of course, in their early teens, they found their own-aged friends and activities.

Very early in life, Armen Jr. showed signs of genius – especially in music – just like his dad. Don't laugh. In the late seventies, I formed a local musical group which included my nephews as the musicians and me, as the singer. We played at weddings, picnics, and church gatherings and I sang in ten different languages – even ones that I did not speak, such as Farsi, Greek and Italian. I just memorized the words and the tunes. I had a brilliant nephew who arranged and conducted *all* our music. We practiced constantly and we became quite popular. However, all good things don't last forever. As they grew older, the nephews followed their own careers. One pursued medicine. The other chose to be a professional musician, and the last two (brothers) became successful automotive businessmen. There went the band.... *Ah, the good old days!*

I said *all that* to say that Armen Jr. followed in his dad's footsteps, in music. At the age of three, he began piano lessons. Twelve years later, in high school soccer, he shattered a kneecap into five pieces. While incapacitated and bed-ridden for a solid month, he mastered playing the guitar. At the age of sixteen, he attended USC on a scholastic scholarship and majored in Television Communications.

He now works for K-CAL (Channel 9) in Sports

Broadcasting. In late-night television sports, you may see his name in the credits. At the age of twenty seven, he is an accomplished musician who also leads our worship and praise band at church. In his late teens, he formed a popular local band, *Greensboro Ln.*, cut records and played at many Los Angeles and Orange County night clubs, such as the *Roxy*, *Whisky a Go-Go* and the *Boogie*.

In 2001, within a week of the tragic attack on the Twin Towers of the World Trade Center, he wrote and sang an emotional tribute that is both spiritual and patriotic. If you want a copy, let me know. Even though the band had a good local following, it dissolved shortly after. I believe God's calling on him was *so* great that he traded his rock 'n roll pop music for Gospel compositions to honor and praise our Lord, Jesus Christ. In return, God has blessed him mightily with a good wife, a new home, a great job, and just recently, a beautiful baby girl, *my* granddaughter Kayla.

Speaking of his wife, it is no coincidence that Junior chose and married a pretty *blonde* named Jennifer. My wife Jeannie *finally* got her girl, Jennifer...after all those years.

That brings us to the one who was to be our Jen...Aram. This second child was born in 1981. He had the cutest curly blond hair you'd ever seen. This girl-to-be boy was *never* meant to be a girl. He is also musically talented (he's the drummer in our church worship band), but his *forté* was sports.

Sure, Armen also played little league, and soccer in high school, but Aram *excelled* in sports. Not to brag much, he lettered in three sports while at Canyon High School, winning many honors in baseball, football and soccer (of course). He was extremely popular in school, as he was chosen "King of Homecoming Court" and Commissioner of Pep Rallies. A graduate of Chapman University, majoring in Kinesiology, he now manages a fitness center, where he also works as a personal trainer and a physical therapist.

He is one buffed dude.

He lives at home, and Mom and I like it that way. To this day, he thrills us with his athletic prowess. Long after high school and college athletics, Aram dabbles in organized sports with his long time friends. Just this week, his team won a local dodge ball championship, second year in a row. And last night, we witnessed an exciting intercity softball championship win. As he came home later that night, I greeted him at the door with a kiss, thanking him for *all* the wonderful years he has thrilled us in sports.

Enough about the kids! Let me get to the woman of my life. I have loved this lady since I laid eyes on her on the steps of St. Joseph's Church, back in 1959. We married in 1967, and ever since, she has been my soul mate. Very much like my mother, this woman has been the spiritual backbone of *our* family. Yes, I worked and put food on the table. But she put order in our lives. She presented me with two wonderful boys.   She has picked up after me relentlessly for 39 years, fed me, clothe me, loved me, through thick and thin, through good times and bad, through sickness and health. And not one murmur.

I've always said that being a mother and wife is the most difficult job a woman can have.

She has taken care of us three boys, even in her weakest moments. She is truly a MOM, one that sees after our family unequivocally and unilaterally, asking nothing in return. She reads her Bible day and night, and prays over the family's welfare, asking God's favor upon her loved ones. That's all she asks in this world, for she knows well her position in this modern age. And she knows well her place in the next, with all the rewards that God has stored up for her. I am *truly* blessed to have such an angel.

Sometimes I think I don't deserve her. Being an Armenian, I'm childish and demanding. I need to be served "hand and foot." And she does that, without complaining.

She knows what I need before I ask for it.

You might say I'm a chauvinist. But I choose to believe that she knows God's word well enough to know that the man is the head of the household, and he is to be served, honored and respected. This may not sit well with the so-called feminist movement. No wonder we have 75% broken homes and divorces, *just* in California.

I'm not suggesting that a woman slave over her husband. *Not at all.* I equally respect and honor my wife, and I take care of *all* her needs. I know my place in life, according to God's law – not man's. And my wife *chooses* to serve me, and I love her dearly for that.

Do you know that I *honestly* do not even know the size of my shoes, shirts or pants? I don't. She has bought all my clothing ever since we've been married. *Without her I'm nothing. With her I am whole.*

Thank you, Lord, for sending me a guardian angel. My biggest fault is that I don't often enough tell her how much I love and appreciate her. I'm not romantic in that way. I don't bring her flowers every week. I don't buy her gifts and presents too often. But she has everything she needs. She has my credit cards. What *else* does she need? Seriously though, she knows my heart. She *knows* how much I love her.

We would not have lasted nearly 40 years if there was no love in our marriage. In *all* that time, we have *only* been apart ten or twelve days, and the bulk of that happened last month when she visited her cousins in New York. Don't think she didn't call me twice a day. What did she think I was going to be doing...? ...Looking for my clothes?

Besides me, God has blessed my wife with great gifts: her two boys, and recently her great joy, Kayla, our granddaughter. It seems her only mission in life now is to please her son and daughter-in-law by babysitting Kayla. At the ring of the telephone, she's out the door driving 45 miles through the maddening traffic to hold her sweet grandchild.

Oh that Kayla! She has brought so much joy into our lives. I can't wait for Sundays just to hold her in my arms. What a proud *dédé* I am. My wife is the *néné*. These are old Armenian terms for endearing grandparents. *And we are that.* In my classroom, next to the pictures of my students, I proudly display Kayla's photos, from birth to date. All my students are familiar with her and they share my joy as I speak about her.

I would be remiss if I did not briefly speak about my twin sister, Zarouhi. She's not immediate family; she's closer than that. She was the youngest of the triplets. As I explained before, we lost the middle child soon after birth. As a youngster, I used to be called by my middle name, Zareh (yes, another Armenian king's namesake). And my sister was called Zaroog (an Armenian diminutive). After marriage, her husband Levon shortened it to *Zar*. She is the only female of the five living siblings and I love her dearly.

Growing up, we were inseparable. My parents and close relatives used a very catchy, whimsical rhyme about us: *Zareh/Zaroog, yergoo moog,* which translated into... Zareh/Zaroog, the two little mice. We laughed together, cried together and even hurt together. I felt her pain as she felt mine. To this day she has this keen sense of discernment. She'll call to make me confess what is ailing me. And she's right 99.9% of the time.

She has a benevolent and philanthropic husband, five charming and personable children, and nine beautiful grandchildren that keep her extremely busy. She is *truly* a warmhearted and giving person. After all these years, we're still very close, even though she's got the money and I've got the brains... er, looks.

While I'm at it, let me mention that I love my three older brothers – Vagharsh, Ardash and Shavarsh – dearly. While we may have had our minor differences (which brothers don't), we worked side by side for over thirty-five years. We're together at all family gatherings and come to each other's aid when necessary. Our extended family numbers just about sixty. You can imagine what it's like at weddings, christenings and anniversaries....

I have spoken briefly about my Dad, *eem hyrig*. I just want to add that he had a great love for his family and wanted the best for his children. He was a mentor to us all. He was a man with deep convictions. He *so* loved Armenia even though he *never* set foot on its "free" soil. He refused to visit his Homeland as long as it was in the hands of the Communist. Sadly, he passed away *before* the fall of Communism, when Armenia once again became independent. *Hyrig* was loved and respected by the whole Armenian community as its Patriarch.

I need to elaborate about my Mom, *eem myrig*. I have dedicated this book to her for many reasons. Of course, the old *cliché*: "Without her I would not be here today." More importantly, as I look back now, well after her demise, I see a saint. During the war, almost single-handedly, she reared five small children.

You would understand the true meaning of that if you comprehend the Middle Eastern culture. She was an exemplary mother and wife. Seldom did she complain. She knew her role in life and embraced it.

In that Middle East and later in the United States, she was the backbone of the family. Mom not only took care of our family, but also any one else in need. She would actually perform minor medical surgery on the sick, young and old. Both in Amman and New York, people would come from miles around for "Dr. Veron's healing touch." If I were to show you the razor marks (to extract infected blood) on my back to cure my severe flu at age 8, you would panic. We had her stop her "practice" in California by threatening to call the police ....

She was revered in the Armenian community of Orange County as its Matriarch. She attended the Armenian Apostolic Church religiously and read her Armenian Bible daily. She was loved by all, simply for her goodness. She did not demand anything in life but prayed for the welfare and well being of her children, and grandchildren, who *absolutely* adored her. *That says it all.* She handled each and every one of life's challenges with honor and a strong belief in God. She will be remembered for her dedication to her family, Church, the Armenian Community and God. There is no doubt that she is in heaven with *hyrig* today.

Here's a funny story about *myrig* and me. When we had that first Armenian Church built in Orange

136

County in the mid-eighties, all the Keuilian Families attended it. After all, we built it with blood, sweat and tears, *and a whole lot of our money* – a donation of a quarter of a million dollars, to be exact. Therefore, once we attended that Armenian Church, we would have to... for life. After doing so for many years, my immediate family – wife, children and I – moved away from the area. Furthermore, the liturgy, at the services, was conducted totally in Armenian. My wife and children could not understand much of it. And the drive was not worth it. It made attending church on Sundays very difficult, especially with two young children.

All right, I'll tell you the *real* reason... At this church, my wife and I could not focus on following the church services. *Our* aim was to worship God. However, there were too many other distractions. Let's leave it at that. Therefore, we set out to look for a new place of worship, closer to home.

Are you ready for another miracle? It was exactly at this time (late eighties) when that serial killer, Richard Ramirez, entered homes through open windows and, in the name of Satan, viciously killed his victims. This had a profound psychological affect on Armen Jr., ten years old at the time. He was not *at all* able to sleep alone in his room at nights; I had to hold him tightly *all through the night*. This went on for weeks; it made my life miserable, for lack of sleep. The slightest release of my arms would awaken him. Nothing that Mom and I said or did would diminish his fears.

This went on for months, since the "night stalker" was still at large. We searched for spiritual guidance. We called Jeannie's godfather, Frank, who still lived in Florida. He directed us to a Full Gospel Church and advised us to invite the pastor to exorcise the house. He felt that the room was demonized.

*To the point...*the Pastor showed up, prayed over the house and in Junior's room in particular. He prayed over the youngster as well.

That very night and every night thereafter, the little guy slept "like a baby", in his own bed.

That, my friend, is a Miracle with a capital "M", for the killer was not yet captured for another few months. To whom do *you* turn in time of need, when *man* can't solve your problems...?

Needless to say, we began attending this pastor's local Full Gospel Church.

Getting back to the funny anecdote with my mom, it did not please her at all that we changed churches. Even though this new church was Christian, it was Protestant. To her it might as well have been atheist. "You sold your soul to the devil", she would cry out in disgust. *"Asdvadzet pokhetsir.* You changed your God". "But Mom," I'd assure her, "it's the very same God in another place. After all, He is everywhere." *"Vrass mi khntar, lagod.* "Don't try to patronize me, you twerp." She would continue, "I was reading the Bible before you were born." She always knew how to put me in my place.

Myrig was getting on in her years and her health was failing. After *hyrig* passed away, she really began to "lose it". Every one of us, her sons and daughter, wanted to take her in to live with us. She adamantly refused. She did not want to leave her modest house, neighborhood and close friends – as if we were moving her to another state. One time, we bodily forced her out of her house, against her will. She almost died, crying like a baby. So, we gave up the idea....

We all took turns visiting her house, especially her beloved grandchildren, Troy, Karin, Raffi, Silva, Armen, Maral, Sosy, Chris, Shant, Arax, Talin, Tamar, Lara, Armen Jr. and Aram.

At every visit to her house, I'd ask her if she was ready to go. "*Badrasd ess, myrig jon*?" "*Oor gertamgor*? Where am I going?" She'd get annoyed, "*Noren eskessar*...there you go again...." I just wanted to make sure that Mom was saved, that she had accepted Jesus Christ as her Savior, and that she was going to heaven. In case...that's all. Oh, in the back of my mind, I was *sure* she was.

She died peacefully one afternoon, on the phone, talking to one of her granddaughters. I assure you that she's in heaven *right now* laughing off her statements about my trading my God. For she knows there is only *one true, Omnipresent God. Park Asdoodzo.* Praise God.

Chapter Twenty Six

Come Fly with Me

Ever since childhood, I wanted to visit Western Europe, and France in particular.

Oh là là... la France. La Tour Eiffel, L'arc de Triomphe, Les Champs Elysées, etc.

In my youth, in the Middle East, we were too poor to travel even outside of Amman, Jordan, except for yearly visits to relatives in Jerusalem. Similarly, we were too busy in New York, just trying to survive. In California, we were too involved in raising our families and building a business. Yes, on occasions, we'd vacation in Hawaii or Bermuda. But that's all.

However, when I began teaching at El Rancho in 1997, the opportunity presented itself to see Western Europe. One of my colleagues, Mr. Pitts, organized yearly trips for 30-40 students to Russia, France, England, Spain, Italy, Germany and Greece. The kids were thrilled to see el Prado in Madrid, il Colosseo in Rome, le Louvre in Paris, the Parthenon in Athens, Westminster Abbey in London, and much, much more. *The pages of History, English and Art books came alive with every visit.*

Unfortunately, it all came to an abrupt end after September 11, 2001. Americans were a target even *before* the hideous attacks on the Twin Towers in New York, the Pentagon in Washington D.C., and United 93 (over Pennsylvania), headed for the White House.

Last night, I viewed the movie *United 93*, the true story about the brave Americans who thwarted the plan (and destination) of the 4th hijacked plane on that fateful day. I couldn't help but cry, and yet be so proud of those American passengers who sacrificed their lives to save...the White House and possibly the President.

For the first time, Americans lost their freedom to travel abroad without fear and to carry on business as usual at home. Nowadays, we're always on guard, looking over our shoulders. We teach our children to be a little more cautious, to be alive, alert, awake, and aware at all times. "Take nothing for granted. Be vigilant." It has truly changed our lives. America is not used to this kind of imprisonment. But we're learning to live with it, as some countries *do* in Western Europe, Asia and the Middle East. Nevertheless, I want to thank Mr. Pitts for realizing my lifelong dream of seeing that part of the world, at least.

Chapter Twenty Seven

Getting To Know Me

To know me well, you need to know what I like and dislike. I love kids, music, pizza, reading, and sports. I dislike hatred, oppression, and rap music.

I've spoken plenty about kids; you *know* how I feel. I left a lucrative job in the corporate world to be around people I love. Enough said. Music is a universal language and I'm into languages. Music propels my world – morning, noon and night. Armenian music is my favorite (duh). I also enjoy Middle Eastern melodies, Arabic and Persian in particular. *La musique francaise, la música española*, and *mousikē Graikos* (Greek) are captivating. Lately, students, like Sana, Puneet and Shivani, have introduced me to Indian music – very refreshing.

Let's not forget the 50's and 60's *rock 'n roll* – the King, Elvis and the Foursome, the Beatles. They absolutely revolutionized the music genre. I'm proud to say that I saw Elvis in concert at the Anaheim Convention Center and have made a pilgrimage to Graceland after his untimely demise. I know by heart every popular Elvis tune you can name.

I also witnessed the first ever "Invasion of America" by the Beatles at JFK Airport in New York in 1963. We waited until midnight for the plane to land. Upon arrival, the plane taxied and stopped in the middle of the runway. A limousine approached and *whisked* them away before you could blurt out, *"She loves you, yeah, yeah, yeah."*

I am also infatuated by Country and Western Music. I've got to tell you that one of my former students, Hadeah Kanbar, having graduated high school, has just cut a CD and sent me a copy with her younger sister. *Mark my words.* Hadeah is gonna be a Country Star. She has the most soothing voice and the prettiest smile.

My wife and I just got back from a Kris Kristofferson concert, and we will see Dwight Yoakum next week. I'm also a great fan of the legends: Johnny Cash, Marty Robbins, Merle Haggard and George Jones. Hey, I don't own a pick-up truck, drink whiskey or hang out at honky-tonk saloons; I just enjoy listening to the lyrics and the melody. Call me a redneck, I don't know. Just the other day, one of my friends at church asked, "what do you get when you play a country western record backwards? You get your wife back, your life back, your pick-up truck back...."

I mentioned Armenian music as my favorite only because *Hye yem yes (I am an Armenian),* and I have listened to it since birth. In my early youth, I heard nothing but folk and patriotic songs that told of our ancestors' plight under Turkish domination. They were usually sad songs that lamented over persecution and the loss of precious loved ones in the battles for freedom. The patriotic songs eulogized our heroic freedom fighters who made the ultimate sacrifice (gave up their lives) to save Armenia from the hands of the oppressors. Nowadays, one local but profound singer, Karnig Sarkissian, brings audiences to tears with his interpretive and expressive voice.

In the late sixties, a new genre in music took hold. Much like American Rock 'n Roll was embraced by the American youth, this new modern sound became very popular with the Armenian youth. It was lively and carefree, and "you can dance to it". A new flock of pop singers sprung and sang about youthful love. *Adiss, Maxim, Paul, Harout* and others, to this day, pack dinner and dance halls with young people (and old), looking for fun – dancing the night away. The old theme of lamentation had shifted to jubilation.

Older Armenian music distinguished itself through its unusual tempo and unique instruments. In its music one wouldn't normally find 1/2 or 3/4 time; and among its instruments, one would find the *doumbeg* and the *oud*. The former is an hourglass-shaped drum (with tightly drawn pigskin atop), held between the legs and beat by fingers and palms of both hands. The latter is a half-large-watermelon-shaped-rounded-back guitar, which has unique resonance and acoustics that make the sound fuller, and exotic in many ways. This instrument is used by many Middle

Eastern countries, including Arabia.

Speaking of Arabia, my second favorite is Arabic music, sung by the likes of Fareed Al Atrash and Abdel Halim Hafez. The former is a masterful *oud* player and singer, the Frank Sinatra of *all* of Arabia in the fifties and sixties. The latter was heir apparent.

I love French music as well. Enrico Macias, Charles Aznavour and Edith Piaf have thrilled me for over a half a century with their love songs and pity-full interpretation of their lives and of the world. *C'est la vie.* That's life in *French* for you. Macias, however, is an Algerian born Jewish/Frenchman who champions the cause of children, and peace in the Middle East in his music. *A man after my own heart.*

Finally, I'm fond of Spanish music. The flamenco flavored love songs of Julio Iglesias (no, *not* his son Enrico) move me. I'm not *too* crazy about mariachi music. However, there are a few very popular Mexican songs that I teach my students – the likes of *Cielito Lindo* and *De Colores.*

While on the subject of music, what is this total infatuation of our young people with rappers and "teenie queenies"..? Where, when and why did our society loosen its stronghold on decency, respect, honor and integrity? When did *degradation* of women and *anarchism* become acceptable? Have we sold our souls for the almighty dollar? Are these "musicians" our children's idols and role models?

It sure seems so, from the billions of dollars

spent on CD's, DVD's and related accessories. Never mind the clothing (or lack thereof) they exhibit. Our kids passionately mimic every lewd and lascivious move and gesture of their favorite artists – even at school dances and performances – as if they're at a concert.

I know what I'm talking about. During school, I have confiscated a few students' CD's with most profane lyrics an *adult* would be embarrassed to hear. When did we agree that filth, obscenity and nudity shall rule our very being?

Can we talk honestly here? In the name of liberty and freedom, *we* have allowed the pollution of the minds of our children. *We* have discarded modesty and purity and embraced indecency and immorality.

PARENTS, WAKE UP!!! Mom, do you know what your child is doing in the "privacy" of her room, let alone outside with "friends"? Why is this apathy and indifference? Are you too busy or too afraid to discipline your child? Where's your obligation as a guardian? Or are you afraid of losing your status as your child's "best friend"? Best friends don't allow one another to delve into the path of deterioration and destruction. Get a hold of your child; teach her right from wrong. She's *screaming* for guidance and help.

Save your child, for Christ's sake. After all, you happen to be older and much wiser. "Oh, it's harmless," you say. "There's no need to overreact. She'll outgrow the fad. Or, maybe one day, she may even become a *star* in her own right...." Alas, what a price to pay – to sell one's soul for money, fame and power! For in the Gospel of Luke, Jesus laments, *"What good is it if you have it all, but have sold your soul to the devil?"*

I don't want to scare you or tell you anything you don't already know. But have you checked the rate of teenage pregnancies and drug abuse lately? I wonder where they learned that from….

I'm sincerely sorry to yell at you so, but our kids are *too* precious to lose to drugs.

Speaking of drugs, on a very serious note, Mom and Dad, if you have a loved one who has given into the lifestyle of alcohol and drugs, and you think that it's too late, all is lost and nothing can be done to save the situation…. *IT IS NOT TOO LATE.* Last Sunday, a group of "reformed junkies" (teenagers and older) came to our church and gave individual testimonies on how they have completely overcome their addiction to weed, pot, meths, crack, heroine, speed, cocaine, alcohol, etc. They have turned their lives around through a loving and caring organization called Teen Challenge. If you have tried other means and the effort has failed, you owe it to yourself and your child to visit the website, www.teenchallenge.com. There is *no cost* for the help, and the success rate is phenomenal (over 85%). Anyone who makes a strong commitment will be accepted into the program. Call me. I'll put you in contact with management. You can thank me later.

FOOD! I love Armenian food! My mother was absolutely the best when it came to making *dolma* and *sarma*: eggplants, peppers and grape leaves, stuffed with cooked ground meat and rice. Have you tried *boereg*: chopped meat and grilled onions inside thin, overlapped, fried dough? What about *Koefta:* extremely fine, uncooked, minced meat, mixed with wheat, and molded into palm-size pieces, dipped in diced parsley?

Have you ever tasted *lahmajoon*, Armenian pizza, the kind Nellie's (my wife's best friend) mom makes? Right out of the oven – hot and spicy. And don't let anyone tell you it's Arabic or Greek. That also holds true for *bakhlava*, a scrumptious Armenian delicacy that goes great with Armenian coffee.

Don't get me wrong. Occasionally, I *do* eat a hot dog or a cheeseburger with fries. After all, *yes Amerigatsi yem*, I am an American. However, my eating unhealthy food doesn't sit well with my nutritionist son, Aram.

I encourage all my students to read. *Read anything decent; just read.* Reading will transport you into the past and "back to the future" within moments. It's knowledge at your fingertips. My favorite two books are *The Bible* and the recently written best seller, *The Da Vinci Code*.

Whoa! You may be saying, "what a hypocrite! This Bible-thumping Christian names that heretical book as a favorite...." Before you get bent way out of shape, Dan Brown, the author, is a brilliant writer *and* a Christian. Secondly, the book is **fiction.** One cannot deny that the novel is beautifully written. The movie, however, did not do justice to the book, even though I admire the leading actors in it.

As a Christian, strong in your own conviction, you take what you want and discard what is contradictory to your belief. Do you believe every thing you read?

You know my preference in sports. Soccer, called *football* in the rest of the world, is an obsession with me. I've made my feelings known earlier about this great pastime which is beneficial (healthwise) to the young and old, male and female. When I don't play, I officiate. I'm quite involved in the sport in that I'm the president of a local referee association in North Orange County. Yes, I *do* like other sports. I'm a Yankee fan way back from the days of Mickey Mantle, Roger Maris and Yogi Berra. Fifteen years ago, I took my family on an East Coast vacation, where we visited many baseball parks and watched as many games as possible.

Occasionally, I go to the stadium of the *"Anaheim Angels of Los Angeles"*, especially when the Bronx Bombers are in town. I go to the "Pond" (Honda Center) when the Ducks play hockey. I was a loyal fan of the Los Angeles Rams when they occupied the Big "A" in Anaheim. Badminton and roller derby aren't my thing. Sorry. The Lakers, however, *are* my team, through thick and thin. Years ago, the Magic Man (and James) thrilled us all with "Showtime", as did Shaq and Kobe recently. Lately though, things aren't so hot, but I'm not ready to jump ship, yet. There's always next year....

Epilogue

My Parting Words

I often tell my students that my job is not just to teach the subject matter. That's an instructor's job. I consider myself first a teacher, a teacher of life and values, as well as Spanish and French. I believe that 99.9% of parents, regardless of their religious beliefs, *do* want good, family values instilled in their children by well-educated, honorable and mature teachers. Not every instructor is a teacher.

Previously, I mentioned the qualities of a good teacher. An instructor is not necessarily a teacher, and it takes more than a special instructor to *be* a teacher. It takes that *special* kind of person to become that one, who himself is disciplined, experienced, knowledgeable, mature, and with a good amount of love in his heart. Love for kids – that Agape love that comes from God for *all* children of race, color and creed. In the eyes of the Lord, children are a special gift sent to us, to us *all* – not just to the parents – to teach, guide and love as our own, for the short time that we have them.

I have a great responsibility. As a teacher, I have been commissioned to love and protect the children. God's command is "not to harm even the *least* of my brethren…, but to 'suffer' the little children to come unto me…" to love and teach and protect (my own understanding of the Bible verses).

Yes, it took me forty years to realize my true calling. And God can call anyone, even an old and otherwise useless business man like me – with humble beginnings – to be a vessel for *His* work and *His* glory. He'll do the same for you. All He asks is that you are obedient to His Word. He'll do the rest; He'll reward you for your willingness and availability.

So this is what *my* life is all about. "Taking care of children" is my priority. In my golden years, I plan to retire (within six years) and enjoy the happy moments of "growing up" with our granddaughter, Kayla, and any other children God blesses our kids to have. I pray that my wife will be beside me to enjoy those special moments.

Of course, soccer will *still* be my pastime, Lord willing. I plan to referee games until I make it to that great, big, *futbol* field in the sky…with new knees.

Ah yes, and I'll *still* be serving Jesus Christ while here on earth…*and* come to the aid of anyone in need. For *that* is my mission in life.

May God bless you! And hey, thanks for listening.

Here are a few of Mr. K's quips and their meanings, some original, some borrowed:

1. 99.9 44/100% of the time----------"Almost always".

2. Look alive, alert, awake and aware---------- Be "focused" in and out of the classroom.

3. Put *that* in your pipe and smoke it----- Think about *that* for a while.

4. Hey, *gumba* (Italian) ------------- Short for gumbare, "friend".

5. No ticky, no shirty-------------- If you haven't done the h/w, you *can't* take the test.

6. Marry rich!--------------------- If you keep on this course, you won't be able to support yourself....

7. Friends, Romans, Countrymen, lend me your ears (Shakespeare) ------Hey kids, pay attention, please.

8. That excuse *plus* a $1.75 will buy you the best cup of coffee and a donut at Dee's Donuts------Your "excuse" is *worthless*.

9. Spanish and French are languages of agreement-- Verbs agree with subjects in number; adjectives agree with nouns, in gender and number.

10. "Homey" don't play that----------------I don't allow the retake of failed exams... more than once.

11. When in Rome, do as the Romans do--------In my class, do it my way.

12. You can lead a horse to water, but you can't make him drink-------- *You* have to be receptive to my teaching.

My Mother and Father at their 50th Wedding Anniversary party in 1984. "Hyrig " soon passed away in 1986 and "Myrig" was taken in 1999.

The love of my life Jeannie, my wife of almost 40 years.
Some one asked, "how does F-O-R-T-Y years feel?" Just like 4
minutes...underwater!!!!
Oh, just kidding. I love her with all my heart for the wonderful,
caring person that she is.

From left, my twin sister Zaroug, Shavarsh, myself, Vagharsh
and Ardash. This was taken at my 50th Birthday "surprise"
Party" (10/1/1996)

Kayla Keuilian, my granddaughter and my life !!!
Yeah, she's also a Yankee fan... We start 'em young ...

BEFORE
1948 in the rubbles of
Amman, Jordan. My twin
sister Zaroug and I,
in Arabic garb.

MY TWIN SIS

AFTER
During intersession 2001
in my classroom at El
Rancho during
"Show and Tell". Actually,
my sister surprised me
during class,
I was teaching HISTORY

A 2004 picture of my wife Jeannie, to my left, and my sons Aram and Armen Jr with his wife Jen.

2005, 40th Yr. High School Reunion in California "Best Buddies" from Cardinal Hayes H.S. in the Bronx, New York.
Left to right: Billy White, Maurice Masson, Armen Keuilian and Dr. Rick Luceri …A little older and a little fuller.

My mentor, good friend and fellow referee, Dr. Harvey Grody, near a soccer field before a game.

Two former students ("hotties"), Allen Cadreau and Michael Shuff, visiting Mr. K at an Eighth Grade Promotion Night at El Rancho. They promoted in 2002 and I clearly remember that the girls wouldn't leave them alone.

To Mr. K,
The best and most memorable teacher I've ever had. Thank you for your support!

Lots of love,
Hadeah Kanbar

For More Information, please contact:
(714) 313-2772 or (714) 280-8207
email: LKanbar@sbcglobal.net

Hadeah Kanbar, a 2001 El Rancho graduate.
She sings Country !!!

Sarah Lovett, a June 2006 graduate, in my classroom. She has an unforgettable smile.

To a fellow referee. Asal Alipanah

Asal Alipanah, on the last day of the 2006 year. A wonderful student <u>and</u> a fellow referee. There's <u>always</u> a smile on her face.

Two of my former students Noelle and Kristine who came to help me transfer food and supplies to Arquero, Ronald McDonald House at one of our Builder's Club outings.

Form 1-415
TREASURY DEPARTMENT

UNITED STATES DEPARTMENT OF JUSTICE
Immigration and Naturalization Service
(Rev. 12-21-51)

MANIFEST No

MANIFEST OF IN-BOUND PASSENGERS (ALIENS)

Class TOURIST from Pireaus GREECE June 3th 1956

" QUEEN FREDERICA " .... arriving at port of New-York,N.Y Jun 25th 1956
Name of vessel

Line No.	Family Name Given Name	Immi Ser. No. Extension	Immigration Department or Ports of Entry	Date of Entry and Port of Arrival, Steamer, and Line Number
1	KEUILIAN	Man well	I-888451 Jordan ian		203
2	KEUILIAN	Vir mika	I-88645: Jordan ian		
3	KEUILIAN	Vag aretnk	I-88645: Jordan ian		
4	KEUILIAN	Ard uheeo	I-888451 Jordan ian		
5	KEUILIAN	Shw arah	I-88845' Jordan ian		
6	KEUILIAN	Arm n-Garik	I-86884:7 Jordan ian		
7	KEUILIAN	Zar ukhi	I-868451 Jordan ian		
8	KOLLATSOS	Nicolas	I-646065 Greek		
9	KOMSTNAKAS	Kyri akos	I-646981 Greek		
10	KONDOLIOS	Ilias	I-646456 Greek		
11	KONSTANTOPOULOS	Ourr min	I-646247 Greek		
12	KONSTANTOPOULOS	Nicholas	USpp 9325 Greece		
13	KOPETAS	Georgios	I-645666 Greek		
14	KORATSIS	Elias	I-646756 Greek		
15	KORELLIS	Georgios	I-646934 Greek		
16	KORELLIS	Panagoula	I-646933 Greek		
17	KORELLIS	Ipsy anti	I-646935 Greek		
18	KORELLIS	Anastasia	I-646936 Greek		
19	KOSTARIDES (KOSTARIDES)	Vasilios	I-646369 Greek		
20	KORESIOS	Konstantinos	I-690542 Greek		
21	KOUTOUZOS	Sofia	I-583479 Greek		
22	KOUTOUZOS	Ioannis	I-583277 Greek		
23	KOUTCUZOS	Andreas	I-583270 Greek		
24	Closed at line No 23 2nd Purser G.CHIOS c/o More Lines Agency Inc. 42 Brockway N.Y 4 N.Y		USC Aliens Total		
25			107	June 25 1956

1956 Manifest, Queen Frederica

About the Author

Armen Manuel Keuilian was born in the Middle East in 1946. He immigrated to the United States (with his family) as a refugee in 1956. He spent his pre-teen and teen years in New York City while attending parochial school (elementary through high school). In 1966, he, along with his brothers, moved to Orange County, California, where he worked, attended college and raised a family. In 1996, he left the partnership in his brothers' lucrative automotive business to pursue a lifelong dream of teaching children at the middle school level. He's been married faithfully to his wife, Jeannie, for nearly forty years. They have two wonderful boys and a darling granddaughter who is the love of their life. Today, 2006, in his tenth year as a teacher, he yearns to tell his story for the benefit of others, both young and old.